FOR THE RECORD

FOR THE RECORD
THE FIRST WOMEN IN CANADIAN ARCHITECTURE

Edited by Joan Grierson
and the For the Record Committee

 DUNDURN PRESS

Library and Archives Canada Cataloguing in Publication

For the record : the first women in Canadian architecture/edited by Joan Grierson and the For the record committee.

Includes index.
ISBN 978-1-55002-820-1

1. Women architects—Canada—History. 2. Women architects—Canada—Biography. 3. University of Toronto. School of Architecture—Graduate students—Biography. I. Grierson, Joan II. Title.

NA1997.F67 2008   720.92   C2008-900380-2

1 2 3 4 5   12 11 10 09 08

Conseil des Arts du Canada   Canada Council for the Arts   Canada   ONTARIO ARTS COUNCIL CONSEIL DES ARTS DE L'ONTARIO

We acknowledge the support of the **Canada Council for the Arts** and the **Ontario Arts Council** for our publishing program. We also acknowledge the financial support of the **Government of Canada** through the **Book Publishing Industry Development Program** and **The Association for the Export of Canadian Books**, and the **Government of Ontario** through the **Ontario Book Publishers Tax Credit program** and the **Ontario Media Development Corporation.**

Editor: Meg Taylor
Design: Counterpunch/Peter Ross
Printer: Friesens

Opening photographs:
page 1 (left) Residence of Lawren Harris, Toronto, 1933, Alexandra Biriukova, Architect; (right) Royal View Apartments, Edmonton, 1954, Wallbridge and Imrie, Architects.
page 2 (left) Harvie House, Calgary, 1953, Wallbridge and Imrie, Architects; (right) District Office for the Ministry of Natural Resources, Midhurst, Ontario, 1974, Natalie Liacas, Architect.
page 3 (left) Silvano Color Lab, Toronto, 1979, Joanna Ozdowski, Architect; (right) Daymond House, Guelph, 1991, Joan Burt, Architect.
pages 18–19 Plan for an infirmary at the Sir James Whitney School for the Deaf, Belleville, Ontario, 1972, Natalie Liacas, Architect.

Printed and bound in Canada
www.dundurn.com

Dundurn Press
3 Church Street, Suite 500
Toronto, Ontario, Canada
M5E 1M2

Gazelle Book Services Limited
White Cross Mills
High Town, Lancaster, England
LA1 4XS

Dundurn Press
2250 Military Road
Tonawanda, NY
U.S.A. 14150

**To women in Canadian architecture,
past, present and future**

CONTENTS

FOREWORD

The older I get, the more I appreciate those who went before me. The more I learn of their lives and their work, the more I am amazed by their accomplishments and can't help but wonder *how* they did it. We may not be able to retrace the how of much of it, but books such as this tell us *what* they did, and we can draw inspiration and courage from the stories of the women profiled here.

Who encouraged these pioneering women to enter a male-dominated field like architecture? Who told them they could do the job just as well or even better than men? Who mentored them if they wanted to juggle family and career? Maybe it was a family member or someone at school or in the office, or maybe no one did – maybe they just knew they could. But most of us have relied on good advice at crucial points in our lives, and we all need encouragement to be patient, to persevere against the odds.

Where were the role models for women in the 1960s when I decided on a career in architecture? They were few and far between. It was my Latvian immigrant parents, Osvalds and Marta Pupols, and my upbringing in New York City that told me to follow my dream. After that, what can I say? I jumped into the deep end of the pool.

We were six women in the entering class of sixty at the School of Architecture at Cornell University in 1961. Life at school was collegial, but there were no female faculty or adjuncts in those five years. None. Four women in my class dropped out within the first two years, leaving only two of us to graduate in the class of forty.

The university dorms had curfews for women (but not for men), and all female students were required to live in residence. Life in the architectural studio included the usual late nights. Staying out all night (part of the night was not an option) meant risking financial aid and other penalties. Luckily I had the support of residence staff, who would warn me of scheduled fire drills when each person was counted, and I'd be sure to work in my room on those nights. Survival by stealth.

At my first job in an architect's office (summers and later full-time) at Eero Saarinen and Associates/Kevin Roche, John Dinkeloo and Associates, the staff of eighty-plus included only three professional women when I arrived: one technician, one foreign-trained architect and one interior designer. Again, there were no real role models, so I just kept swimming.

In 1974 when my husband and fellow architect, Kiyoshi Matsuzaki, and I began working with Arthur Erickson Architects in Vancouver, I met my first and still-active role model, Cornelia Hahn Oberlander, landscape architect. She showed me how to balance a robust professional career, family and volunteer work – all the while maintaining good humour and a positive outlook.

During the design and construction of the C.K. Choi Building for the Institute of Asian Research at the University of British Columbia in the mid-1990s, I had the exceptional experience of working with a mostly female team. We were determined to take the concept of environmental responsibility as far as it could go. Energy and resource conservation was a primary concern, but the design solution also created a healthy and desirable place to work. Virtually every workstation has a large window that opens and its own temperature controls. Odourless paint, carpets laid without glue and constantly circulating fresh air eliminated the usual toxins found in buildings.

I am convinced that we blossomed in the exceptionally supportive atmosphere that grew out of our weekly gatherings. The result was an environmentally sustainable project well ahead of its time. We all declared our love for nature and our responsibility to future generations. Some of the many sustainable design practices followed in the C.K. Choi Building include the use of recycled building materials, natural ventilation and lighting, and stormwater retention (rainwater storage for irrigation). Water resources are further conserved with composting toilets and a greywater system, which is used to irrigate the surrounding landscape.

At the induction ceremony for newly registered architects in British Columbia in December 1989 a few women spoke of the unreasonable hurdles they had encountered in their education and registration paths. We wondered how widespread these experiences and sentiments were. After some phone calls, eighty women packed into a small meeting room to share their stories – and to demand change. We organized a Saturday workshop in the spring of 1990; with over 100 attendees, this was the beginning of Women in Architecture B.C., a group that is still active. That initial workshop identified common wishes for mentors and support systems that women could easily access, especially for those working in isolation. Over the years this group has been an advocate for change in the professional institutes; provided seminars, tours and newsletters; published the book *Constructing Careers: Profiles of Five Early Women Architects in British Columbia* in 1996; and curated several exhibits.

In 1998, when I became the first woman president of the Royal Architectural Institute of Canada, the RAIC Board agreed to support workshops that would provide a forum for women to exchange information and ideas for change. We asked participants to offer specific recommendations to schools, to professional organizations and to architectural practices on how to make our profession more welcoming to women. From all regions, we heard the need for more female faculty at schools of architecture, more flexibility for women balancing family and careers, more networking opportunities. In many sessions we discussed the possibility of a national organization of Women in Architecture, perhaps under the umbrella of the RAIC. But that remains on our wish list.

As women architects around the world gain in prominence, it's important to acknowledge the women who came before us and to celebrate their trail-blazing courage, passion for design and downright pigheadedness. This is our inheritance. The publication of this book is one more step toward reclaiming our past.

Eva Matsuzaki
Vancouver, October 2007

Since 1984, Eva Matsuzaki has been a principal of Matsuzaki Architects Inc., an award-winning leader in environmentally sensitive design. From 1985 to 1990, she served as an Adjunct Professor in the School of Architecture at the University of British Columbia. From 1974 to 1984, she worked as an associate with Arthur Erickson Architects. Matsuzaki is a founding member of Women in Architecture B.C. and an advocate for women students and practitioners. She was the first woman president of the Royal Architectural Institute of Canada, elected in 1998.

Born in Riga, Latvia, Eva Matsuzaki (née Pupols) holds a B.Arch. degree from Cornell University. After graduation in 1966, she worked in the office of Eero Saarinen and Associates/Kevin Roche, John Dinkeloo and Associates in Connecticut before moving to Vancouver in 1972.

MASONS CONSTRUCTING THE CITY WALL, *Cité des Dames*, Collected Works of Christine de Pisan, fifteenth century, British Library.

PREFACE

Vitruvius, Palladio, Christopher Wren, Thomas Jefferson, Frank Lloyd Wright and Le Corbusier – these are just a few of the many great architects who have been recognized over the centuries. Many kings but no queens. There is a legend that Jane Wren, daughter of Christopher Wren who was charged with the rebuilding of London's churches after the Great Fire of 1666, was responsible during her brief life for work on three Wren churches in east London. By the late nineteenth century, a few women architects had appeared but it was not until the second half of the twentieth century that women entered architecture in significant numbers.

This book is about women in architecture, yesterday and today, and about the establishment in Canada of the profession itself. Prior to 1890, architectural training in Canada was acquired through apprenticeship. Starting that year, courses in architecture were offered at the University of Toronto; in 1896, McGill University in Montreal followed suit. Today, there are eleven architectural programs at universities across the country.

It was from the Department of Architecture at the University of Toronto that Marjorie Hill graduated in 1920, the first "girl architect," as described by a Toronto newspaper at the time. *For the Record* profiles Marjorie Hill and some of the women who followed her. They were among the first women to become architects in Canada.

Although this book focuses on the early women graduates in Architecture at the University of Toronto, three distinguished architects who were trained elsewhere should be mentioned: Catherine Chard Wisnicki, Phyllis Lambert and Blanche Lemco van Ginkel. Above and beyond their design work, these three women have made outstanding contributions to education within the profession.

Catherine Chard Wisnicki was the first woman to graduate in Architecture from McGill, in 1943. She was an active participant in the development of west coast modernism and taught for over twenty years in the School of Architecture at the University of British Columbia until her retirement in 1986.

Phyllis Lambert holds a master's degree in Architecture from the Illinois Institute of Technology and had an award-winning architectural practice based in Montreal. In 1979, she founded the Canadian Centre for Architecture, a museum and international centre for architectural research – based on the conviction that architecture is an urgent public concern.

Blanche Lemco van Ginkel graduated from McGill in Architecture in 1945 and completed her master's degree in City Planning at Harvard five years later. A distinguished educator as well as a successful architect and planner, van Ginkel was Director, then Dean of Architecture at the University of Toronto from 1977 to 1982.

Researched and written by women architects, this book speaks in a collective voice. It is our intention to provide information about the profession of architecture and to follow the part that women have played in it from the early years. That there have been many changes over time is apparent in the final chapter, which presents the work of six women architects working today, selected from across the country.

It has taken us twenty years to publish this book, the same length of time Marjorie Hill had to wait to practice architecture. We bow to her patience and fortitude.

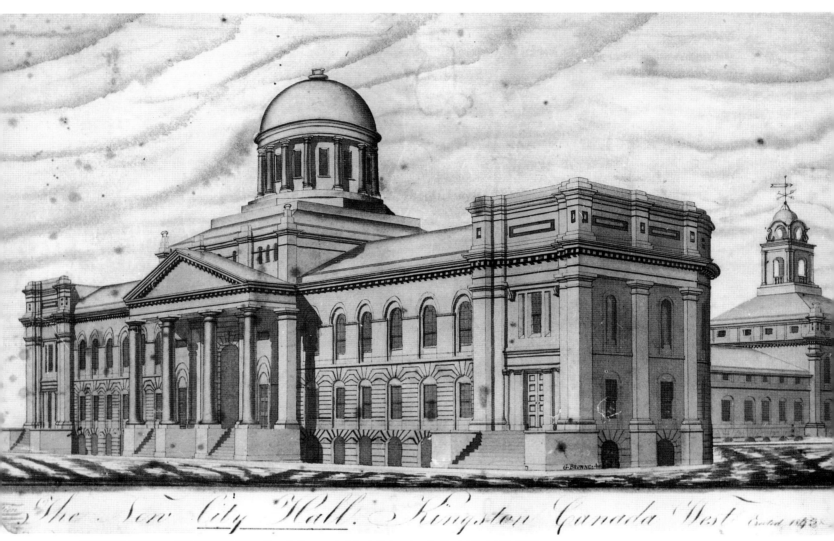

The New City Hall, Kingston Canada West Erected 1843

KINGSTON CITY HALL AND MARKET, 1840, George Browne, Architect. Watercolour by Harriet Cartright, 1844.

A SHORT HISTORY OF EARLY WOMEN IN ARCHITECTURE

When Marjorie Hill graduated in 1920 as Canada's "first girl architect," she was entering a profession that was in its infancy here, having been established only thirty years earlier, in 1890. In the years leading up to that date, when this country was known as British North America, building was done by settlers, carpenters and masons, as well as the military. Over the course of the nineteenth century, railways were laid out, trade increased and settlements grew in size and number. Montreal, Kingston, Toronto and Halifax all became important centres, while the west remained the realm of the fur trade.

In 1853, an extraordinary woman appeared in the west. Mother Joseph travelled with other Sisters of Providence from Montreal to Washington Territory and to Fort Vancouver. Their mission was to establish hospitals and schools, providing care for native children, the elderly and the poor. Providence Academy in Vancouver was completed in 1883, and by that time Mother Joseph had designed, raised funds and supervised the construction of seventeen facilities in the area. The American Institute of Architects later honoured her as the "first architect of the Pacific Northwest."

The settlements in the east were steadily growing. In 1841, the union of Upper and Lower Canada – Ontario and Quebec – had created the Province of Canada. For three years it was thought that Kingston would serve as the capital, during which time an international competition was announced for the design of a new city hall and market. The call for proposals resulted in thirteen submissions, one of which came from Sarah Turton Glegg, daughter of a building contractor in Kingston and friend of Toronto architect John Howard, who also submitted a proposal. Neither Glegg, about whom nothing more is known, nor Howard was successful; the council chose the design of Montreal and Kingston architect George Browne.

This was a time when architects brought their skills from abroad. In Canada, the only training available was through apprenticeship. When the same George Browne emigrated from Ireland in 1832, he started a school in Quebec City – open only to men – where drafting skills and knowledge could be acquired for $4 a month. Architects prepared drawings, wrote specifications, reviewed construction costs and certified payments. For such services they received a fee of 5 percent, based on the cost of construction. Few architects could afford to do only this and survive financially. Expanding settlements were surrounded by wilderness, however, and there was a continuing need for canals, bridges, roads and railways. An architect could keep busy as a surveyor, builder, developer and engineer.

John Howard understood this. He brought his training as an architect and surveyor from England, arriving in 1832 in Muddy York, which was soon to become Toronto. Howard was, at various times, surveyor, city engineer, public notary and farmer. For twenty-three years, he was the drawing master at Upper Canada College. He also produced architectural drawings for commissions that came his way.

Mechanics Institutes – established by local philanthropists and based on a British model – began to appear, providing the working populace with resources necessary for the study of technical subjects. British and American pattern books containing architectural designs were frequently consulted by those involved with the building trade in Canada; professional journals, illustrating recent work abroad, arrived by ship within weeks of publication in England.

In 1851, the opening of the Crystal Palace in London, England, caused much excitement. Its iron-and-glass construction opened up a world of design possibilities; it could be dismantled and relocated. The building demonstrated the use of new materials, new ideas and new design. Variations on the structure soon began to appear elsewhere. In 1858, the Palace of Industry was

CRYSTAL PALACE, London, England, 1850–1851, designed by Joseph Paxton; **CRYSTAL PALACE,** Exhibition Park, Toronto, 1879, Strickland and Symons, Architects.

constructed in Toronto in three months, using iron, wood and glass that had been fabricated locally. After the close of the trade exposition, the Palace of Industry was dismantled and then rebuilt, with a third floor added, in Exhibition Park not far from its original location. This grand new structure was called the Crystal Palace, and opened the first Toronto Exhibition in September 1879. Regrettably, it was destroyed by fire in 1906.

The Industrial Age was well under way. Railway expansion required iron foundries, locomotive shops and rolling mills. Burgeoning industry and commerce called for new types of buildings: factories, railway stations, hotels and office buildings. The office building had a natural walk-up limit of four to six storeys, but by 1856, with advances in building technology, the creation of new materials and the invention of the Otis elevator, that limit could be extended. In Canada, this taller type of building, with its system of cast-iron columns, beams and masonry walls, first appeared in 1888: the ten-storey Montreal headquarters of New York Life Assurance, designed by Babb, Cook and Willard, Architects, of New York.

In 1860, structural steel became available, and somewhat later reinforced concrete, well suited to large-scale structures, bridges and dams, came into common use. These new systems of building, new techniques of construction and unfamiliar building materials, not to mention competition from American firms, put great stress on practicing architects in Canada.

New York architect Bruce Price, who had been commissioned to design Windsor Station in Montreal, soon became the favourite architect of the Canadian Pacific Railway. Other Price commissions include the original Banff Springs Hotel and the Château Frontenac in Quebec City. Richard Waite, a Buffalo architect, worked north of the border as well, designing buildings for Canada Life and for the Canadian Bank of Commerce between 1880 and 1895. Waite was a juror in a closed competition for the design of the Ontario Legislature, and it was he who came away with the commission that resulted in Queen's Park in Toronto.

New building systems and materials required advanced technical knowledge that could not be learned through apprenticeship. Students were leaving the country to gain experience in Boston, Chicago, even London, England. In 1873, the Ontario legislature had called for the creation of the School of Practical Science, and by 1878 it was offering three-year diplomas in mining, engineering, mechanics and manufacturing. In 1889, the School became

CHÂTEAU FRONTENAC, Quebec City, 1893, Bruce Price, Architect; **CANADIAN BANK OF COMMERCE,** Dawson City, Yukon, 1901, in the Beaux-Arts style.

affiliated with the University of Toronto. The following year, the first courses in architecture were offered as part of the university curriculum. These courses included basic engineering and design in the Beaux-Arts style.

The Ontario Association of Architects, incorporated in 1890, controlled entry into the profession and set standards for the province. Quebec followed suit later the same year. A new trade magazine was launched, *The Canadian Architect and Builder.*

While the profession was becoming established, so was the country. With the British North America Act of 1867, the former colonies entered into Confederation to become the Dominion of Canada with a population of 3.5 million. To unite the country, the government promised to build a transcontinental railway and provide ferry service to Prince Edward Island.

In 1885, after five years' construction, the transcontinental railway was completed, and the country was connected coast to coast. At the western terminus, Vancouver prospered, and Winnipeg – halfway across the country – became a major business centre. Settlements appeared along the rail lines. To keep pace with this growth, the Bank of Commerce shipped prefabricated banks to new towns atop flatbed rail cars, two rail cars per bank.

In 1906, a new branch was being erected somewhere in the Prairies every other week.

Most of the population still lived on farms, but towns were growing and the shift had begun to urban life. Larger towns boasted modern conveniences such as gas-powered and horse-drawn trams; theatres were well attended and the level of culture, over all, was on the rise. Women worked with church groups and benevolent societies for the welfare of women working in factories and the homeless and in the realm of medical care. To promote better practical education for wives and mothers, Adelaide Hunter Hoodless established the first Women's Institute in Stoney Creek, Ontario, in 1897. Other socially minded groups were forming, too: the Women's Christian Temperance Union, the Women's Suffrage Society of Canada and the Young Women's Christian Association.

Women were becoming a force. They wanted more say in matters that concerned them, and it was easy to see that political power and education were both essential to that purpose. Victoria College, in Cobourg, Ontario, opened its doors to women in 1877, and University College in Toronto followed in 1884. Frustrated in attempts to enter established medical schools in Toronto and Kingston, women managed to start their own schools in both cities. The earliest

WOMEN'S BUILDING, WORLD'S COLUMBIAN EXPOSITION, Chicago, designed by Sophie Hayden, 1893; **HOTEL LAFAYETTE,** Buffalo, New York, 1904, Louise Blanchard Bethune, AIA.

professional degrees accessible to women were in the fields of science, pharmacy, law and eventually medicine. Architecture was still in the future.

In Europe and in the United States, it was a different story. In 1881, in Buffalo, New York, Louise Blanchard Bethune opened an architectural office at the age of twenty-five. She had learned her trade in the office of Richard Waite, the man whose commissions included the Ontario Legislature. With R.A. Bethune, her husband and her partner in the firm, Louise Blanchard Bethune shared a practice that was responsible for the design of many of Buffalo's early educational, industrial and commercial buildings – including Hotel Lafayette (1898–1904), a city landmark.

In 1880, the first woman graduated in architecture from Cornell University in Ithaca, New York. By 1891, when women were invited to compete for the design of the Women's Building for the World's Columbian Exposition (Chicago World's Fair), there were thirteen entrants from around the United States. First prize went to Sophie Hayden, a twenty-one-year-old graduate of the Massachusetts Institute of Technology. It is interesting to note that Louise Blanchard Bethune refused to enter this competition because the honorarium for the winner of the women's competi-

tion was one-tenth that being offered for an equivalent competition open to male architects.

In the 1894 MIT graduating class in architecture were three women; one was Marion Mahony. From 1895 to 1909, she worked with Frank Lloyd Wright in his Oak Park Studio outside Chicago. When she started, she was twenty-four and Wright was twenty-eight. Mahony married Walter Burley Griffin in 1911; their architectural firm built an international reputation. On the west coast, in 1904, architect Julia Morgan opened an office in San Francisco. Before retiring in 1951, she had designed over 700 buildings. By 1910, Julia Morgan was one of fifty women architects practicing in the United States.

In Europe, too, women were active in the profession. Emilie Winkelmann opened her own office in 1908 in Berlin, with a staff of fifteen prior to the First World War. In Austria, the first woman architect began a practice in 1917. Margarete Schütte-Lihotzky worked on Frankfurt Social Housing with Ernst May: her work produced the Frankfurt Kitchen, a prefabricated unit that could be inserted into high-rise apartments by a crane. (Ten thousand such units were installed between 1925 and 1930.)

In Finland, Signe Hornborg graduated from the Polytechnic

BERKELEY WOMEN'S CITY CLUB, Berkeley, California, 1929–1930, Julia Morgan, Architect; **MUELLER HOUSE**, Chicago, Illinois, 1910, Walter Burley Griffin and Marion Mahony Griffin, Architects.

Institute of Helsinki in 1890. In England, Ethel Charles was the first woman to graduate from an architectural program in 1898. The following year, the Royal Institute of British Architects elected by a single vote to admit women, and Ethel Charles joined the RIBA. In 1900, they admitted a second woman: Bessie Ada Charles, Ethel's sister. In Australia, Florence Taylor was the first woman to graduate in architecture in 1907. Before coming to Canada, Alexandra Biriukova completed degrees in Petrograd in 1914 and in Rome in 1925.

Women's interest in architecture was growing. In the United States, it led to an unusual school of architecture and landscape design exclusively for women. The Cambridge School was close to Harvard, which did not admit women. A Radcliffe College graduate requested tutorials in architectural design in the office of Henry Frost and his partner. Several more women applied, and the office turned into a school. That was in 1917. When the school closed twenty-six years later, 500 women had been trained and the Cambridge School had a well-established reputation for excellence.

In Canada, it was a different story, with only limited signs of interest. In Montreal, in the 1890s, Jean Eleanor Howden studied at McGill University for two years, but when she was told a woman could not be granted a degree in architecture, she left the university and joined the office of Edward and W.S. Maxwell, Architects. In 1908, one woman's application to study architecture was referred to the McGill University Faculty of Applied Science, which decided it "would not be advisable to admit women at the present." McGill relented in 1937. Women architects were slow to appear in Canada and few in number. Mary Anna Kentner enrolled in 1916 at the University of Toronto, and Marjorie Hill, who had first enrolled in Alberta, graduated from the University of Toronto in 1920.

That was the beginning. It was in 1917 that women in Canada won the right to vote. Five years after Hill graduated, for the first time in history, a young woman took her seat in the House of Commons in Ottawa. Agnes Macphail was to be the only woman there for fifteen of her nineteen years in office, but as she said, "A woman's place is where she wants to be."

The first women who trained to be architects in Canada would certainly agree. Between 1920 and 1960 twenty-eight women went through the School of Architecture at the University of Toronto. The following pages describe their professional lives, with glimpses of the times they faced upon graduation.

WOMEN GRADUATES IN ARCHITECTURE

1920 TO 1960, UNIVERSITY OF TORONTO

THE 1920s

EVENTS

- The League of Nations convenes in Paris.
- William Lyon Mackenzie King is prime minister of Canada.
- In the Soviet Union, Vladimir Lenin dies at 53. Joseph Stalin takes control.
- Military leader Chiang Kai-shek becomes leader of the Republic of China.
- Adolf Hitler publishes *Mein Kampf*.
- Calvin Coolidge becomes U.S. president on the death of Warren G. Harding.
- The discovery of insulin is announced at the University of Toronto.
- First transatlantic telephone communication and first network radio broadcast.
- First transmission of television.
- Charles Lindbergh flies solo across the Atlantic.
- Air mail service begins in northern Canada.
- October 29, 1929, Black Tuesday, the stock market crash marks the start of the Great Depression.

LIFE

This decade is known as the Roaring Twenties. Women bob their hair and smoke in public. The flapper dress appears and the Charleston hits the dance floor. Movies, radio and the gramophone replace vaudeville and bring entertainment into the home.

- Flying is all the rage. Eileen Vollick of Hamilton, Ontario, is the first woman pilot to take off and land a plane on skis.
- Agnes Macphail, an independent candidate from Grey County, Ontario, is the first elected woman to sit in the House of Commons.
- The marketplace introduces strained baby foods and the first motel.

(LEFT) MODEL T FORD 1922 TOURING CAR. By 1927 the Ford Motor Co. had produced 15 million automobiles. **(TOP) WASSILY CHAIR,** designed at the Bauhaus by Hungarian-born Marcel Lajos Breuer in 1926, manufactured by Vienna's Gebrüder Thonet.

(LEFT TO RIGHT) HOUSES OF PARLIAMENT, Ottawa, Ontario, 1916–1927, Pearson & Marchand, Architects; **EDMONTON PUBLIC LIBRARY**, Edmonton, Alberta, 1923, G.M. MacDonald and H.A. Magoon, Architects; **PLAN OF THE GARDEN VILLAGE FOR DOMINION STEEL PRODUCTS CO.**, of Brantford, Ontario, 1923, Greta Gray, Architect, AIA.

STATISTICS

1921 POPULATION OF CANADA 8,787,949 Population of U.S. 105,710,620
In the 1920s the urban population in Canada surpassed that of the rural areas.
Architecture graduates in Canada **3 WOMEN** 135 men

BOOKS *Jalna* by Mazo de la Roche; *The Waste Land* by T.S. Eliot; *Winnie the Pooh* by A.A. Milne.

FILMS *The Gold Rush*, starring Charlie Chaplin; *The Jazz Singer*, starring Al Jolson; *Nanook of the North*, the first feature-length documentary.

RADIO Sports; Will Rogers; the Metropolitan Opera.

MUSIC Bessie Smith records the blues; Louis "Satchmo" Armstrong joins King Oliver's jazz band; George Gershwin composes *Rhapsody in Blue*.

ART Emily Carr exhibits at the National Gallery and begins an association with the Group of Seven.

ARCHITECTURE

In Canada in the 1920s, Beaux-Arts Neoclassicism and the Gothic Revival continued to dominate architectural design, especially for public buildings such as Union Station in Toronto, the Edmonton Public Library, and the Parliament Buildings in Ottawa. This was all about to change.

The modernist movement in architecture was initiated by a small group of architects in Europe, among them Walter Gropius and Ludwig Mies van der Rohe in Germany, Le Corbusier in France, and J.J. Oud in Holland. In 1919, Gropius founded the Bauhaus, a design school that sought to relate art and architecture to technology and the practical needs of modern life. In 1923, Le Corbusier wrote *Vers une architecture*

(Towards a New Architecture), advocating functional design, honest use of materials and basic geometric shapes. (In Canada, the igloo would have met these requirements.)

In England, Elisabeth Whitworth Scott won the 1928 international competition for the Shakespeare Memorial Theatre in Stratford-upon-Avon. It was the first major public building in England to achieve a dignified effect without recourse to historical sources. Women were making an appearance as planners as well; the MIT-educated architect Greta Gray designed a garden village for the workers at Dominion Steel in Brantford, Ontario, as early as 1923.

In Canada, new ideas in design were absorbed slowly, with historical styles continuing to dominate. There were six schools of architecture in Canada at this time. At the University of Toronto, architecture was a four-year course with graduating classes of less than ten students; the degree granted was a Bachelor of Science until 1923, when it became a Bachelor of Architecture. That same year, Eric Arthur joined the staff from England and began to develop the curriculum in a more contemporary direction. In 1928, the course was lengthened to five years.

Marjorie Hill had enrolled in architecture in 1916 at the University of Alberta. When the school closed during the First World War, she transferred to the University of Toronto and set a record in 1920 as the first woman in Canada to graduate with a degree in architecture.

(LEFT TO RIGHT) BAUHAUS BUILDING, Dessau, Germany, 1926, workshop wing on the right, Walter Gropius, Architect; **SHAKESPEARE MEMORIAL THEATRE**, Stratford-upon-Avon, England, 1929–1932, Elisabeth Whitworth Scott, Architect.

MARJORIE HILL

B.A. 1916, B.A.Sc. 1920

1916 B.A., University of Alberta.
1916–1918 University of Alberta, first two years in the School of Architecture.
1918–1920 University of Toronto, third and fourth years in the Department of Architecture.
1920 B.A.Sc. (Architecture), University of Toronto. Worked at Eaton's department store in interior design.
1921 Applied unsuccessfully to register with Alberta Association of Architects. Taught in a rural school in Alberta.
1922 Worked at MacDonald and Magoon, Architects, Edmonton: work included a Carnegie library in Edmonton. Returned to University of Toronto for postgraduate studies in town planning.
1923–1928 Moved to New York for summer design course at Columbia University, followed by work with architects Marcia Mead and Katherine Budd.

1925 Registered, Alberta Association of Architects.
1928–1929 Returned to office of MacDonald and Magoon, Architects, in Edmonton.
1930 No architectural work was available. Marjorie Hill turned to weaving and glove making, teaching these crafts through the Depression.
1936 Moved to Victoria, British Columbia, where she became a master weaver.
1940 Architectural commissions led to part-time practice: residential renovations and conversion of houses to apartments.
1945–1963 Architectural practice continued after the war: houses, motel addition, fellowship hall, hospital.
1945 Elected to Victoria Town Planning Commission.
1953 Registered, Architectural Institute of British Columbia.

"One must have artistic talent, practical experience, professional knowledge, good business sense and executive ability, resourcefulness and a determination to persevere. With these assets, there is no reason why a woman should not be as successful as a man." (*Toronto Star,* June 15, 1920)

"The principal product of a handicraft program should be better people ... Heredity, attention to diet, no smoking or drinking, lots of music and reading the papers keeps me going." (*Vancouver Sun,* May 29, 1984)

CONVOCATION AT UNIVERSITY OF TORONTO, 1920. Front page of *Toronto Star* on June 15, 1920. "Miss E.M. Hill is ... the first woman to graduate from the School of Architecture."

1963 Retired after twenty-eight years of architectural practice. Continued to teach weaving and produce works for sale: "I am fully occupied with congenial and satisfying tasks."

1985 Marjorie Hill died at the age of eighty-nine in Victoria.

(RIGHT) 10-SUITE APARTMENT, Fort Street, Victoria, B.C., 1954.

(BELOW) GLENWARREN LODGE, Balmoral Avenue, Victoria, B.C., a 63-bed private hospital, 1962. (There were subsequent additions.) (Left) main floor plan.

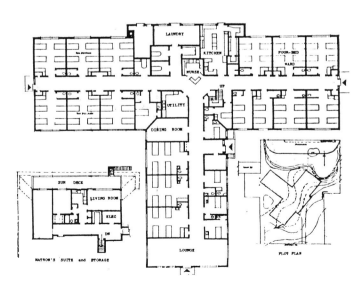

JEAN HALL

B.Arch. 1923

1917 University of Toronto, completed first year in general arts. Enrolled at School of Architecture.

1919–1921 Interrupted studies after second year to teach in Rearville, Alberta. After two years, returned to university.

1923 B.Arch., University of Toronto.

1923–1927 Employed as an artist doing wash drawings and watercolour by Toronto art firm.

1925 Architectural commission – a fourplex – for her father, a Toronto builder.

1927 Employed by Workmen's Compensation Board, Toronto, processing medical claims.

1958 Retired from Workmen's Compensation Board.

1982 Jean Hall died at the age of eighty-six in Toronto.

Toward the end of First World War, an appeal was made to university students to volunteer as teachers in the Canadian Prairies. Jean Hall and her sister, a medical student, were among those who responded. Jean was sent to Rearville, east of Calgary. Because there was no accommodation for the new teacher, the residents built a sod house for her.

In the years following graduation, Jean Hall tried repeatedly to find work in an architectural office. By 1931, the effects of the Depression were widespread – her father's construction firm was one of many forced to close. According to her sister, Jean was disappointed that she had been unable to have a career in architecture. For all that, she may still have been the first Canadian woman graduate in architecture to have seen a building of her design actually built.

U OF T ARCHITECTURAL CLUB, 1922, executive vice-president Jean Hall (centre).

(TOP) FOURPLEX,
63 Jerome Street,
Toronto, 1925;
(left) floor plan of
first floor.

(LEFT) JEAN HALL
outside her sod
house in Alberta,
1919–1921.

**(RIGHT) WAR
MEMORIAL,** student
work, 1923.

ELIZABETH LALOR HARDING

B.Arch. 1927

1927 B.Arch., University of Toronto.
1927–1930 Worked in the office of William Lyon Somerville, Architect, Toronto: residential work.
1930 Married American architect Carrol Harding and moved to Weston, Massachusetts.

1941 Worked in the office of Page and Steele, Architects, Toronto, then returned to Boston, Massachusetts. Records are incomplete.
1958 Married George P. Carlton.
1961 Elizabeth Carlton died in Peterborough, New Hampshire, at the age of sixty-one.

In 1929, while working in Toronto, "Betty" Lalor spoke at the Art Gallery of Toronto on the development of a Canadian style in architecture. The same year, she worked independently on the conversion of a farmhouse to a summer residence on Lake Joseph in the Muskoka region of Ontario. The project was published in the July 1929 issue of *Canadian Homes and Gardens*.

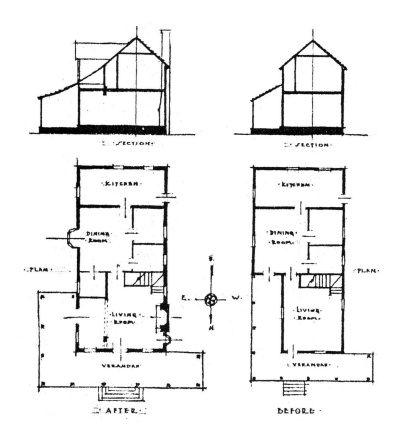

(TOP LEFT) SMALL BREAKFAST DORMER in the sloping east roof features shelves and cupboards to hold dishes and serving trays.

(TOP RIGHT) FARMHOUSE renovation plans.

(OPPOSITE AND RIGHT) DRAWINGS OF THE OLD FARMHOUSE "before" (opposite) and "after" (right). "The chief problems presented to the architect were to enlarge the living room to a size in keeping with summer hospitality, to provide greater verandah space and to create a more interesting exterior. The roofline was lowered, the small balcony moved to the side, the verandah now offers a more spacious welcome and the use of small-paned windows softened the general aspect of the house." (*Canadian Homes and Gardens*, July 1929)

THE 1930s

EVENTS

- The devastating effects of the Depression are widespread. The numbers of jobless soar, and there are demonstrations in London, New York and Paris.
- Mackenzie King returns as prime minister in 1935, after his Liberal party defeats R.B. Bennett and the Conservatives.
- Franklin Roosevelt is president of the United States.
- Joseph Stalin purges thousands of dissidents.
- In 1936, the Spanish Civil War erupts.
- In 1937, the Japanese intensify their invasion of eastern China.
- Adolf Hitler is made chancellor of Germany. He annexes Austria, Sudetenland and Czechoslovakia before invading Poland.
- September 3, 1939, Great Britain and France declare war on Germany; Canada declares war a week later.

LIFE

This is a hard-times decade, without unemployment insurance, universal health care or welfare. The Canadian Broadcasting Corporation (CBC) is established in 1936: radio offers some escape into the world of entertainers, game shows, soaps and music. Jazz gives way to swing, with the big bands of Guy Lombardo, Count Basie, Benny Goodman and Duke Ellington.

- Drive-in movies, laundromats, sliced bread, Skippy peanut butter and Superman appear.
- Women claim a place in the sky: Amelia Earhart solos the Atlantic, flying from west to east, and Beryl Markham follows suit, east to west. Skater Cecile Smith of Canada is runner-up to world champion Sonja Henie.
- Cairine Wilson and Iva Fallis are the first Canadian women to be appointed to the Senate.

(LEFT) 1937 VW PROTOTYPE VEHICLE. Volkswagen, the "people's car," designed by Ferdinand Porsche. **(TOP) HARDOY OR BUTTERFLY CHAIR,** designed by Jorge Ferrari-Harding for Grupo Austral, 1938.

(LEFT TO RIGHT) CAPITOL THEATRE and office building, Halifax, Nova Scotia, 1930, Murray Brown, Architect; **MARINE BUILDING,** Vancouver, 1930, McCarter and Nairne, Architects; **RESIDENCE OF LAWREN HARRIS,** Toronto, 1933, Alexandra Biriukova, Architect.

BOOKS *Such Is My Beloved* by Morley Callaghan; *The Good Earth* by Pearl S. Buck; *The Grapes of Wrath* by John Steinbeck.
FILMS *The Silent Enemy*, a film about the Ojibway of Northern Ontario battling hunger; *The Wizard of Oz*, starring Judy Garland.
RADIO *The Happy Gang* on CBC; Orson Welles's *War of the Worlds*.
MUSIC Guy Lombardo and the Royal Canadians; "Anything Goes" by Cole Porter; "Brother Can You Spare a Dime?" by Jay Gorney and E.Y. Harburg.
THEATRE Royal Winnipeg Ballet founded.
ART Canadian Group of Painters (including Lawren Harris, A.J. Casson and A.Y. Jackson) grows out of the Group of Seven.

ARCHITECTURE

The Depression had a devastating effect on the profession in the years leading up to the Second World War. As early as 1931, architectural offices in Canada had reduced their staffs drastically, and many architects were out of work.

In the world of design, modern architecture made a name for itself at the Stockholm Exhibition of 1930. It became recognized not only in Europe but in the Soviet Union and the United States. In 1932, the Museum of Modern Art in New York held an exhibit titled *The International Style*, which introduced modern architecture to the American public. The next year the Chicago World's Fair opened, marking a "Century of Progress." The buildings were described as a shock to the middle-aged, but to the young, a measure of the future. The New York World's Fair in 1939 gave further impetus to modernism.

In Europe, the Bauhaus, now headed by Ludwig Mies van der Rohe, moved to Berlin in 1933 but within months was closed by the Nazi government. Its members dispersed but continued to teach, in England and in the United States.

It was also in the 1930s that modernism reached Canada. Commercial and residential work responded more wholeheartedly than corporate and government establishments, where historical styles were still preferred as an expression of power and tradition. Office buildings were becoming higher and higher. The tallest building in the British Empire in 1931 was the Canadian Bank of Commerce tower in Toronto.

The Dominion Housing Act was passed, followed by a nationwide competition for low-cost housing. On the West Coast, innovative residential work was beginning to appear.

In 1939, the University of British Columbia established a school of architecture headed by Fred Lasserre, an advocate of the International Style. Across Canada during the 1930s, a total of 16 women graduated with a degree in architecture from the following schools: University of Alberta, 3; University of Manitoba, 9; University of Toronto, 4.

(**LEFT TO RIGHT) BOURDON HOUSE,** Sillery, Quebec, 1934, Robert Blatter, Architect; **CANADIAN BANK OF COMMERCE** head office, Toronto, 1931, York & Sawyer, Architects (New York) with Darling & Pearson, Architects (Toronto); **THOMSON BUILDING,** Timmins, Ontario, 1939, H. Sheppard & G. Masson, Architects, the birthplace of the Thomson newspaper empire.

BEATRICE CENTNER DAVIDSON

B.Arch. 1930, M.Arch. 1937

1930 B.Arch., University of Toronto. Toronto Architectural Guild Bronze Medal.
1931 Worked in the office of a German architect in Jerusalem.
1932–1935 Postgraduate studies, School of Architecture, University of Toronto.
1935–1937 Intermittent professional work in the architectural office of P.A. Deacon and Professor Eric Arthur; factory job in a jewellery firm.
1937 M.Arch., University of Toronto – a delay in the granting of her degree was attributed by Davidson to the "radical modern design" of her thesis. Secretary to the first Ontario Committee on Housing. Married Harry Davidson.
1938–1942 Two children born.
1940 on Independent work: architectural negotiator of her husband's land-development

business. Designed two houses in Toronto; designed furniture for family and friends. An *ex officio* member of the jury for the design of the new city hall. Volunteer research assistant to Eric Arthur during the writing of his book *No Mean City*.
1986 Beatrice Davidson died at the age of seventy-seven in Toronto.

"My architectural education did more for me than anything else in any way. It made me open my eyes and led me into a constantly expanding world.

"There was a tradition for those students who won the Guild Medal being offered employment by a certain firm. When I won, however, my lack of experience on the construction site was cited as sufficient reason to break with tradition. I was told to return in five years with proof of experience and then I would be hired – as long as I signed an agreement not to marry for another ten years."

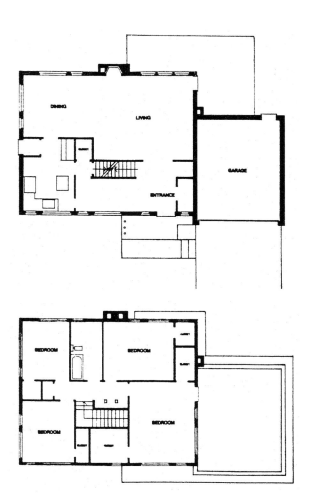

(OPPOSITE, FROM TOP) 1930 FOURTH-YEAR ARCHITECTURE STUDENTS
AND STAFF. Beatrice Centner is fourth from the left. CHAIR, contemporary
design adapted by Davidson.

(ABOVE) DAVIDSON RESIDENCE, Cortleigh Boulevard, Toronto, 1942; plans
showing the first and second floors.

(RIGHT) DINING AND SERVING TABLES, contemporary design adapted
by Davidson.

KATHARINE JEFFERYS HELM

School of Architecture, University of Toronto 1928–1932

1932 Completed four years of study and design thesis at School of Architecture, University of Toronto.

1932–1936 Sales clerk at Eaton's department store in Toronto.

1937 With Edward Helm, a Hungarian officer and toolmaker, travelled to Tahiti, where they married and planned to settle on a plantation. Wrote articles about life in the South Seas for the Toronto *Telegram*.

1937 As war tensions increase, the Helms returned to Toronto. Research for a history of Peel County.

1941–1945 Worked as engineering draftsman with Canadian Industries in Windsor, Ontario.

1945 Moved to Los Angeles. Worked as engineering draftsman for a vehicle parts manufacturing firm.

1947 Moved to Eureka, California.

1947–1951 Worked as engineering draftsman, surveyor and mapmaker. Designed and supervised the building of the family house in Kneeland, California. (A second phase was added in 1973.)

1955–1956 Travelled around the world with her husband.

1956–1975 Employed by the office of the State Highway Division, retiring at the age of sixty-seven.

1982 Moved back to Eureka, following the death of her husband.

1993 Katharine Helm died in California.

Katharine Jefferys Helm was the daughter of C.W. Jefferys, well-known Canadian artist and member of the faculty of the School of Architecture, University of Toronto, from 1912 to 1939. While she was at the School of Architecture the length of the course changed from four to five years. There is no record of her graduating; nevertheless, the skills she acquired at university equipped her for thirty-five years of professional life in California.

1932 FOURTH-YEAR ARCHITECTURE STUDENTS AND STAFF. Katharine Jefferys is seated third from right.

DAMA LUMLEY BELL

B.Arch. 1938

1929 Registered in first-year architecture at the University of Toronto; Dama Lumley was already an elementary school teacher.

1934 Completed final year, School of Architecture. Among the nine students in that year, none had acquired the office experience required for graduation.

1935 Worked as a clerk, selling curtains at Eaton's department store in Toronto.

1937 Display manager and consultant on interior decorating at Adams Furniture, a store in Toronto. Worked for John T. Findlay, Architect, St. Thomas, Ontario.

1938 B.Arch., University of Toronto. Travelled to Europe and Ireland.

1940 Married Alfred Bell, a chemical engineer, and moved to Windsor, Ontario, where two sons were born.

1946 Moved to Stratford, Ontario. First president and building chair of the new YWCA/YMCA. Organized the local chapter of the University Women's Club.

1952 First meeting to organize the Stratford Festival was held at the Bell residence, marking the beginning of the Bells' long-term active involvement with the Stratford Theatre Festival.

1960–1977 Juror for the Canadian Housing Design annual competition. Honorary secretary to the Stratford Festival Board. Awarded the Queen's Jubilee Medal.

1979 Member of the Order of Canada is awarded to Dama and Alfred Bell in recognition of their work for the Stratford Festival. They were the first couple to be so honoured.

2001 Dama Lumley Bell died in Stratford, Ontario.

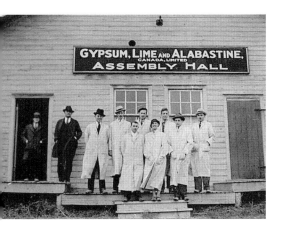

FIELD TRIP to the Gypsum, Lime and Alabastine Company. Dama Lumley is in the front row.

"I have been thinking a lot about my years at the school. It was hard work, sometimes we worked all night – and when the boys went to the burlesque show I would go to a movie or the library. When I think back on that training, I realize it has been invaluable in working with stage designers at Stratford. They have familiar problems to face – time and design and pressure."

When first married and living in Windsor, Dama had the good fortune to meet Eliel Saarinen, the Finnish architect. "He asked if I were married to an architect. When I said 'no,' he shook his head and said, 'no hope.'"

PHYLLIS COOK CARLISLE

B.Arch. 1938

1938 B.Arch., Honours, University of Toronto. Toronto Brick Company award and RAIC Gold Medal (fourth year); Architectural Guild Bronze Medal and Darling and Pearson Prize (fifth year).

1935–1937 Worked in the interior decorating department at Eaton's in Toronto.

1936 Travelled to Norway, Sweden and Italy.

1937 Married Kenneth Carlisle.

1938–1948 Three children born. Independent design work: three summer cabins on Lake Mississauga; private residences in Toronto and Port Credit, Ontario; kitchen designs for Formica. CBC broadcasts on home renovations.

1954 Phyllis Carlisle died at the age of forty-two in Toronto.

The year Phyllis Carlisle graduated, her article about the modern kitchen was published in the December 1938 issue of the *RAIC Journal*. In her conclusion, she stated: "In the rush of modern life, we tend to be oblivious to our daily surroundings. Let us not forget that beauty is to be found not only in the grand and expensive, but should be sought in all things in life, even in humbler places such as the kitchen."

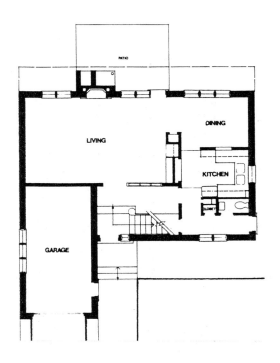

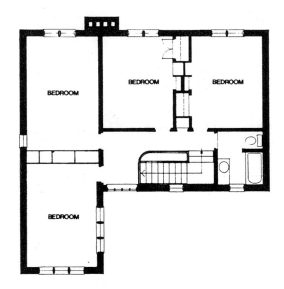

(OPPOSITE, FROM TOP) PHYLLIS COOK AND CLASSMATES at the School of Architecture's annual sketch camp at Gull Lake, near Minden, Ontario, 1934. **ROBB RESIDENCE,** living room.

(LEFT, FROM TOP) ROBB RESIDENCE, Blyth Hill, Toronto, 1952, first and second floor plans.
(RIGHT, FROM TOP) front entrance; back elevation.

ANN GAUTHIER MALOTT

B.Arch. 1938

1937 Completed final year in architecture, but lacked practical experience necessary to graduate.
1937–1939 Worked for the Ontario Department of Public Works in the drafting department.
1938 B.Arch., University of Toronto.
1939 Made plans to tour Europe but reached London just before the outbreak of the Second World War.
1939–1940 Became the first woman hired in the architectural department at Rockefeller Center, New York; work involved office layouts and interior design of the upper eleven floors of the U.S. Rubber Company tower.
1940–1942 Worked in the office of John M. Lyle, Architect, Toronto.
1943 Married Lieutenant Bart Malott, RCOC, in Ottawa.

1943–1946 Assistant chief draftsman and later principal draftsman in the design office of the Federal Inspection Board, Ottawa.
1946 Moved to Toronto when her husband returned from overseas.
1947–1951 Three children born.
1953 Moved to Montreal.

As a student Ann Gauthier had a moment of glory. At the Newman Harvest Festival Dance at the Royal York roof garden her raffle ticket was called. She won a car, a Pontiac Straight-8.

"When the war ended and my husband came home from overseas, I decided to take time out to start a family and a home. I never really went back into practice again."

1956–1962 Through the Montreal Council of Women, Ann Malott became assistant to the organizer of the citizens' committee on low-rental housing. This work led to the Jeanne-Mance public housing project of 1958 in Montreal.

1957–1961 Chair for the Committee on Housing and Community Planning, Montreal Council of Women. Wrote the National Council of Women's brief to the RAIC inquiry into postwar housing in Canada.

1959–1963 Member of the Canadian Housing Design Council.

1989 Ann Gauthier Malott died at the age of seventy-six in Montreal.

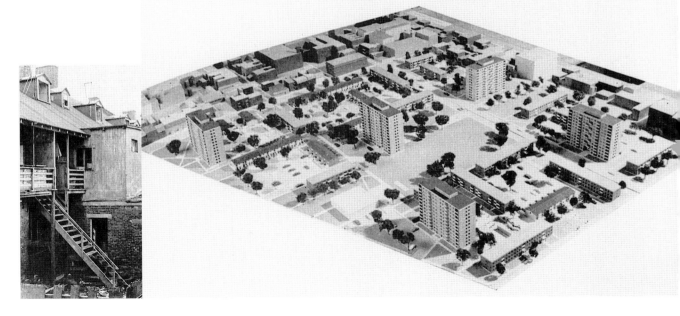

(LEFT) 1939–1940, work with the architectural department at Rockefeller Center on office layouts for the upper eleven floors of the United States Rubber Company tower.

(BELOW) LES HABITATIONS JEANNE-MANCE, Montreal slums (left) were replaced by this major public housing project in 1958.

(OPPOSITE, FROM TOP) 1937 FIFTH-YEAR ARCHITECTURE STUDENTS AND STAFF. Ann Gauthier is in the middle of the front row. **THE GENERAL ELECTRIC PLANT** in Peterborough, Ontario, where Ann Gauthier worked on details for the installation of gun-boring mills and lathes for John M. Lyle, Architect.

THE 1940s

EVENTS

- Winston Churchill becomes prime minister of Britain in 1940; the Battle of Britain rages in the air.
- Japanese bombers attack Pearl Harbor on December 7, 1941. The United States enters the war.
- Allied forces land in Italy on January 22, 1944; on June 6, 1944, the Allies reach the beaches of Normandy.
- Paris is liberated from the Germans, August 25, 1944.
- April 1945, Harry S. Truman becomes president of the U.S.
- Winston Churchill is defeated in British elections in 1945.
- The Second World War comes to an end, with Germany's surrender on VE Day (May 8, 1945) and VJ Day (August 14, 1945), when Japan capitulates after the bombings of Hiroshima and Nagasaki.
- United Nations charter is signed in June 1945.
- May 1948, the state of Israel is established.

- NATO is formed.
- The Soviet Union detonates its first atomic bomb on August 29, 1949.

LIFE

During the Second World War, rationing spreads but prices remain stable, thanks to wage and price controls. Millions are invested in war bonds. Unemployment disappears with new jobs and military enlistment. After the war, the economy continues to grow. Newfoundland joins Canada in 1949.

- Women are mobilized during the war. At Canadian Car and Foundry, Elsie MacGill, Canada's first woman aeronautical engineer, and her staff of 4,500, produce more than 1,400 Hawker Hurricanes for the RAF.
- Skater Barbara Ann Scott wins an Olympic gold medal for Canada in 1948.

(LEFT) 1946 CADILLAC with a two-piece windshield and automatic transmission.
(TOP) MOULDED PLYWOOD LOUNGE CHAIR, designed by Charles Eames in 1945, produced by Herman Miller from 1949.

(LEFT TO RIGHT) SOLAR HOUSE, Dover, Massachustts, 1948, Eleanor Raymond, Architect; **SUNTOP HOMES**, Ardmore, Pennsylvania, quadruple dwelling units, 1940, Frank Lloyd Wright, Architect; **AULANKO HOTEL**, Aulanko, Finland, 1945, Marta Blomstadt, Architect, Matti Lampen, consultant.

STATISTICS

1941 POPULATION OF CANADA 11,506,655 Population of U.S. 131,669,361
Architecture graduates in Canada **34 WOMEN** 267 men

BOOKS *Two Solitudes* by Hugh MacLennan; *Who Has Seen the Wind*
by W.O. Mitchell; *Animal Farm* by George Orwell.
FILM *Citizen Kane*, Orson Welles; *Casablanca*, starring Humphrey
Bogart and Ingrid Bergman.
RADIO Wayne & Shuster on CBC.
MUSIC Glenn Gould debuts with the Toronto Symphony; *Oklahoma!*
and *South Pacific*, Rogers and Hammerstein.
ART In Montreal on August 9, 1948, *Le Refus Global* manifesto is
signed by sixteen artists and intellectuals, including Jean-Paul Riopelle
and Paul-Emile Borduas.

ARCHITECTURE

When the war ended in 1945, new technology honed during wartime
production came into play: moulded plywood was used in furniture
design, and prefabrication and assembly systems were applied to
housing. Non-traditional energy sources including solar heat were
developed. Synthetic materials and new methods of cladding and
weatherproofing become available.

Men and women returning to civilian life required housing and in
many cases further academic training. The federal government established the Central Mortgage and Housing Corporation in 1946. CMHC

was consolidated with Wartime Housing Limited, acquiring about
30,000 houses. These were made available to veterans and their families, and 20,000 more houses were built. New public projects such as
hospitals, airports and schools, which had been put on hold during the
war, led to design and construction innovations.

In the world of architectural design, the acceptance of the International Style was widespread. Walter Gropius, Ludwig Mies van der Rohe
and others from the Bauhaus were teaching in the United States.
Gropius was named chairman of the Department of Architecture at the
Harvard Graduate School of Design, and Mies joined the Illinois Institute of Technology in Chicago. They became role models for several
generations of architectural students.

The number of architectural schools in Canada was reduced to
five with the closing of the University of Alberta program in 1939.
During the 1940s, a total of 34 women graduated with a degree in
architecture from the following schools: University of Manitoba, 9;
University of Toronto, 9; McGill University, 15; École des Beaux Arts,
in Montreal, 1.

When the war ended, first-year enrolment in architecture at the
University of Toronto jumped to 100. The architecture and engineering
first-year students took over a former munitions plant and workers'
housing in Ajax, east of Toronto.

(LEFT TO RIGHT) RED CROSS LODGE, Deer Lodge military hospital, St. James, Manitoba, 1945, Moody and Moore, Architects; **SABA HOUSE,** West Coast, 1948,
Sharp Thompson Berwick & Pratt, designer: Catherine Chard Wisnicki.

MARTHA STEWART LEITCH

B.Arch. 1943, CAA, FRAIC

1938 Enrolled in architecture, University of Toronto.

1942 Married Lieutenant John Leitch, RCE.

1943 B.Arch., University of Toronto. Worked for the City of Toronto Planning Board.

1944 Received British Council travelling scholarship; visited England to study housing and planning.

1946 Worked at Fleury and Arthur, Architects, Toronto.

1947 Founded Leitch Engineering Civil Engineers and Ontario Land Surveyors with her husband.

1948–1956 Four children born.

1955 Faculty of Household Science, University of Toronto, demonstrator (part-time).

1959 Appointed lecturer (part-time).

1964 Appointed assistant professor in the newly formed Faculty of Food Science.

1967 Registered, Ontario Association of Architects.

1968–1975 Assistant dean, Faculty of Food Science, and assistant to the dean, Faculty of Applied Science and Engineering. Registered, Association of Professional Engineers of Ontario.

1970 Death of John Leitch.

1974 Made a fellow of the RAIC, in recognition of community work and for her commitment to the restoration of St. Lawrence Hall in Toronto.

1985 Citizens' award from the APEO (Association of Professional Engineers of Ontario), for community work with Women's College Hospital and Princess Margaret Hospital in Toronto.

2006 Martha Leitch scaled back her professional and community involvements. She continues to live in Toronto.

From the start of her career, Martha Leitch believed that the practice of architecture made a difficult life for a woman. The construction business was competitive, commissions were hard to come by and banks unlikely to help over thin times. In addition, a woman's practice would be restricted by the desire for a family. For all that, she had the desire to stay in the world of the profession, "Come hell or high water."

ARCHITECTURE STUDENTS; Jean Strange and Martha Leitch are seated in the centre.

MARGARET SYNGE DRYER

B.Arch. 1945

1945 B.Arch., Honours, University of Toronto. OAA scholarship (second year); Toronto Brick Prize (fourth year); RAIC Gold Medal (fifth year).

(TOP) WATERCOLOUR by Pegeen Dryer of Toronto houses, 1950s.

1945–1947 Worked at Mathers & Haldenby, Architects, Toronto. Projects included commercial buildings: Campbell Soup building in Simcoe, Ontario; Bell Telephone building; Regent Park Housing redevelopment; and the Parisian Laundry in Toronto.

1948 Married Douglas Dryer, a professor of philosophy at the University of Toronto.

1947–1960 Three children born. Delivered weekly broadcasts for CBC – over fifty segments on residential renovation, house design and community planning.

1950–1951 Worked at Fleury and Arthur Architects, Toronto.

1952–1963 Independent architectural design: houses, residential renovations and additions.

1963 Pegeen Dryer died at the age of forty-two, in Toronto.

One summer, as a student, Pegeen Dryer worked at the City of Toronto Planning Board, and in the years that followed she was active with the Community Planning Association. Her drawings of houses in Toronto's Annex neighbourhood were connected with the Stop the Spadina Expressway campaign of the early 1970s.

(LEFT) REGENT PARK HOUSING REDEVELOPMENT SCHEME OF MATHERS & HALDENBY, 1947. (Left to right) Eric Haldenby, architect; Robert Saunders, mayor of Toronto; and Pegeen Dryer, architect, studying the model.

MARY IMRIE

B.Arch. 1944

1941 B.A. University of Alberta.
1944 B.Arch., University of Toronto. Worked at Harold Smith, Architect, Toronto; C.B.K. Van Norman, Architect, Vancouver. Registered, Alberta Association of Architects.
1944–1945 Worked at Rule, Wynn and Rule, Architects, Edmonton.
1946–1950 Office of the chief architect, City of Edmonton: designed schools and public buildings. (The staff also included architects Jean Wallbridge, University of Alberta '39, and Doris Newlands Tanner, University of Manitoba '44.)
1950 Extended road trip with Jean Wallbridge in South America.
1951 In partnership with Jean Wallbridge, established the firm of Wallbridge and Imrie, Architects, in Edmonton. Early work included commercial buildings, houses and apartments.

1955 Award from the Canadian Housing Design Council, Prairie Region, for Edmonton housing, 1951–1955.
1957 Wallbridge and Imrie built their own office and residence.
1957–1958 Extended trip around the world.
1959 Wallbridge and Imrie practice continued: houses, commercial work, senior citizens housing for province of Alberta and schools for the city of Edmonton.
1979 Offices of Wallbridge and Imrie closed, after twenty-eight years, with the death of Jean Wallbridge.
1980 Mary Imrie designed and built a solar cottage on Lac Ste. Marie, Alberta.
1988 In April, Mary Imrie died at the age of seventy in Edmonton.

"It was hard work with long hours – and the practice could not have supported two families. It was a grind in a cold, hard world. But I would like to add, it was also satisfying and a lot of fun!"

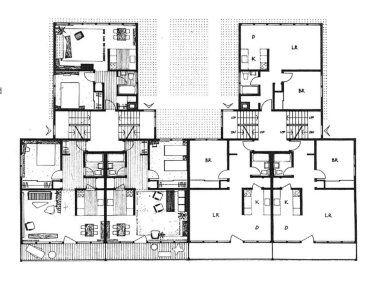

(ABOVE) ROYAL VIEW APARTMENTS, Edmonton, Alberta, 1954, Wallbridge and Imrie, Architects; (right) Royal View floor plan.

(OPPOSITE) "SIX ACRES" RESIDENCE AND OFFICE of Wallbridge and Imrie on the north bank of the Saskatchewan River, Edmonton, 1958.

(ABOVE) MARY IMRIE AND JEAN WALLBRIDGE, Edmonton City architects, visit London, U.K., in 1947 with other architects from Canada and the United States to study town planning and housing conditions.

MARY IMRIE

(RIGHT) HARVIE HOUSE, Calgary, 1953.
The curving porch roof and birch tree mark the
main entrance.

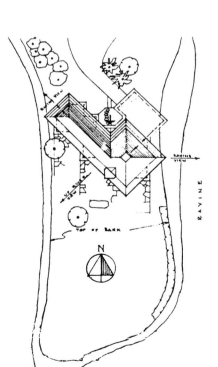

(TOP LEFT) COUNTRY RESIDENCE, West Edmonton,
1963. The site plan (left) shows its location
between two ravines, providing spectacular views;
(below right) ground floor plan.

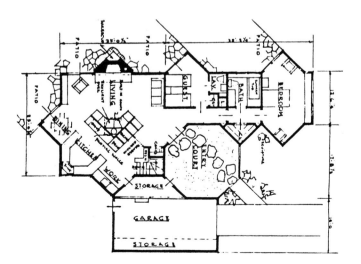

(LEFT) QUEEN MARY APARTMENTS, Edmonton, 1952. Wallbridge and Imrie designed this apartment complex with a courtyard and a central *allée* of evergreen trees.

DALE HOUSE, Edmonton, 1957. Main façade (left) and entrance on the far right.

MARY IMRIE

GREENFIELD ELEMENTARY SCHOOL, Edmonton, 1969; (below right) floor plan of this open concept school.

(ABOVE) THE MUSIC ROOM at Greenfield.

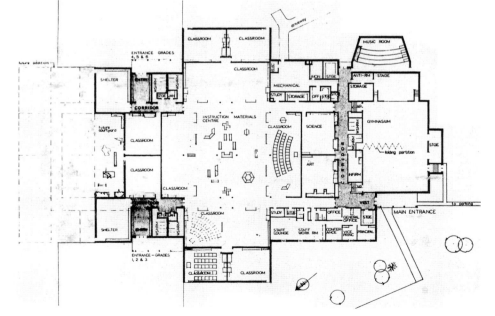

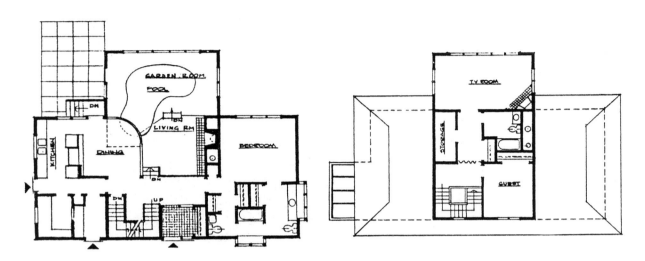

EVERINGTON HOUSE,
Stony Plain, Alberta,
1980, designed by
Mary Imrie after the
death of Jean
Wallbridge. (Top) first
and second floor
plans.

ALICE AYER ALISON

B.Arch 1945, M.Sc. (Preservation Architecture) 1973

1945 B.Arch., University of Toronto. Worked at Page and Steele, Architects, Toronto.

1945–1949 Worked at Mathers & Haldenby, Architects, Toronto. Design and job captain for Wood Green Community Centre; interior perspectives and working drawings for Ontario Research, Queen's Park and Campbell Soup Company, Toronto.

1946 Registered, OAA.

1947 Married Gordon Alison. Joined office of Gordon S. Adamson, Architect, Toronto: commercial and residential design work.

1952 Family was transferred to Geneva, Switzerland.

1953–1960 Family moved to Montreal, where two daughters were born. Worked part-time for two years in the office of Paul Lapointe, Architect: Seamen's Union Motel, residential design.

1962–1970 Moved to Toronto. Independent residential design. Worked part-time in the office of Sproatt and Rolph, Architects, for two years. With Isobel Reeves designs two houses, 1964. Secretary of the historic buildings committee of the RAIC; works on book *Historic Buildings of Canada*. Co-chair of Toronto's Friends of the Old City Hall. Research and photography projects with the RAIC's historic buildings committee, with the Ontario Heritage Foundation and with the Architectural Conservancy of Ontario. Designed centennial walks through "old" Toronto, 1967. One of the founders of the Association for Preservation Technology.

1970–1978 Moved to Larchmont, New York. M.Sc. (Restoration and Preservation Architecture), Columbia University, 1973. Drafting for engineering firms (part-time). Worked in the

"In 1947, the architect Gordon Adamson asked me to become a junior partner. A serious illness intervened, however, and then my husband was transferred to Geneva – and after that to Montreal. Later, too, when we lived in Maryland, there was not much architectural work to be found. And so some small-scale architectural work was fitted into full-time real-estate work.

"To an extent I have practiced on my own, but I have certainly been limited on occasion by not being registered in the U.S., by changes of location, by my gender and by the absence of the kind of network that works for an 'old boys' club."

(ABOVE) FIFTH YEAR 1945: (left to right)
Prof. Carswell, Alice Ayer, Herb Agnew,
Prof. Madill, Pegeen Synge and Prof. Murray.

office of Geoffrey Lawford, AIA, for restoration work on Columbia Circle; monument and foot-bridge in Central Park, New York.

1978–1988 Moved to Washington, D.C., then to Maryland. Worked in the office of William O'Neil, AIA, in Silver Spring, Maryland; designer and project manager on warehouse and shopping centre projects. Restoration work on 1890s apartment building. Certifies as real estate agent.

1988 Returned to Canada; designed and supervised building of the Alison house in Terra Cotta, Ontario.

1991 Alice Ayer Alison died at the age of sixty-eight in Toronto.

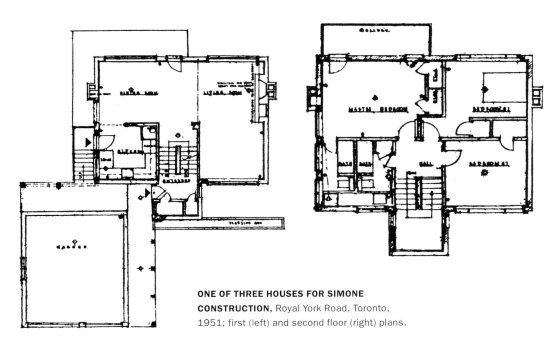

ONE OF THREE HOUSES FOR SIMONE CONSTRUCTION, Royal York Road, Toronto, 1951; first (left) and second floor (right) plans.

ALICE AYER ALISON

W O O D   G R E E N   C O M M U N I T Y   C E N T R E

design by A. Ayer 30,000 sq' community
Sketch by O.S Mathers 1946

(LEFT) WOOD GREEN COMMUNITY CENTRE, Queen Street East, Toronto, 1946. Work with Mathers & Haldenby, Architects: designer and job captain.

ALICE ALISON CAMPAIGNED FOR SEVEN YEARS to preserve Old City Hall in Toronto. This article appeared in the *Star* in 1965. Built in 1899, Old City Hall was finally declared a National Historic Site in 1989.

SHELAGH MACDONNELL ROUNTHWAITE

B.Arch . 1946

1942 Completed two and a half years at the School of Architecture, University of Toronto. Married Lieutenant Frederic Rounthwaite, RCE, an architect.

1942–1944 Lived near army posts in Canada until her husband was sent overseas.

1944 Enrolled in spring term of third-year architecture at the University of Toronto.

1945 Husband returned at end of war.

1946 B.Arch., University of Toronto.

1948–1956 Four children born.

1956–1968 Independent design work.

1969 Entered field of real estate in Toronto. Volunteer work with Girl Guides of Canada, the Royal Ontario Museum and the Architectural Conservancy of Ontario.

1993 Shelagh Rounthwaite cut back her involvement in real estate.

1995 Frederic Rounthwaite died.

1999 Retired.

2002 on Shelagh Rounthwaite joined the editorial board of *For the Record*. She continues to be active.

"My architectural training was an excellent background for the travels we did in the 1970s and 80s. I took many photos – of buildings, not people."

AIMONE HOUSE, German Mills, Thornhill, Ontario, 1968; view of front entrance.

ISOBEL GRACE STEWART

B.Arch. 1946

1940 Completed second-year architecture at the University of Toronto. Married Wing Commander John Young, RCAF, and lives in Nova Scotia until her husband was sent to Newfoundland.

1941 Returned to university, completed the third and half of the fourth year in architecture.

1943 John Maitland Young killed while stationed in Newfoundland; a son was born later that year.

1944 Isobel Young returned to university and finished fourth-year architecture.

1944–1945 Office manager for the town planner, City of Hamilton, Ontario.

1945 Entered her final year at the School of Architecture.

1946 B.Arch., University of Toronto.

1946–1949 Worked for several architects in Hamilton; a few private commissions.

1949 Married real-estate developer Jeffrey Stewart; moved to Oakville, Ontario. Family spent a year in England.

1951–1956 Family returned to Oakville, where three children were born.

1960 Collaborated with her husband, designing houses for a small development. Studied painting; exhibited work.

1964 Visited London, England, taking a course at the Society for the Preservation of Ancient Buildings.

1965–1967 Worked in architectural offices in Oakville, Hamilton and Toronto.

1967 Registered, Ontario Association of Architects.

1967–1973 Established own practice in Oakville: residential work, restoration studies in collaboration with others. Exhibited paintings and photographs. Lectured at the University of Guelph.

"Architecture has changed so much since I started that it is difficult to know what advice to give today. I would suggest that after the first two or three years in the office world, to try and decide what could or would be one's special forte, then try to concentrate on that as much as possible. It's not easy, but I am very happy I was an architect and I really enjoyed it. I also enjoy what I am doing now."

1973 Death of Jeffrey Stewart. Isobel Stewart worked with Parks Department Toronto on historic working farm in Riverdale Park.

1974 Worked for Central Mortgage and Housing Corporation Maritime Office in Halifax, Nova Scotia.

1975 Married horticulturalist Frank Reeves and moved to Toronto.

1980 Designed and supervised the construction of Reeves residence, High Spinney, in Mansfield, Ontario.

1992 Continued painting, photography and glass sculpture.

1994 Death of her husband.

2006 Retired and now lives in Oakville.

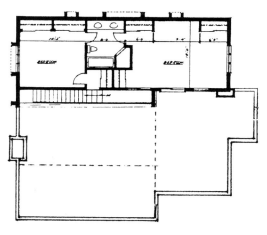

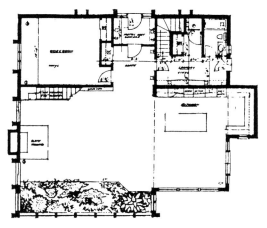

(RIGHT) REEVES RESIDENCE at High Spinney, Mansfield, Ontario, 1980; (above, left) interior view of living room; (right) first and second floor plans.

(OPPOSITE) MURRAY RESIDENCE, Davey Street, Niagara-on-the-Lake, Ontario, 1970.

JEAN TAYLOR STRANGE

B.Arch. 1948

1937 Following schooling in the UK and Switzerland, Jean Taylor enrolled in the architectural course at Brighton Art School and Technical College in England.

1939 After crossing Canada on a six-week trip as a student member of the Overseas Education League, she was prevented from returning to England by the outbreak of war. Enrolled in the School of Architecture, University of Toronto, and was placed in second year with the class of 1943.

1943 Completed the final year of architecture but lacked the twelve months' practical experience required to obtain a degree. In June, entered the Women's Royal Canadian Naval Service, serving in operations and base planning.

1946 Discharged to retirement as lieutenant (SB) WRCNS. Joined Central Mortgage and Housing Corporation office in Ottawa, staff of chief architect Sam Gitterman: drafting room management, housing, community planning and research.

1948 B.Arch., University of Toronto. Attended extension course in subdivision planning, McGill University, Montreal.

1949 Within CMHC was transferred to newly created Housing Research Division, publications section, under Humphrey Carver.

1950 Married Captain William Strange, OBE, CD, RCN.

1955 Appointed assistant to CMHC advisor on housing design, Andrew Hazeland; responsible for publication of housing design books and advice to architects submitting plans. Appointed to CMHC's executive staff course. Member of the judges' committee of the National Industrial Design Council, 1957. Member of Community Planning Association of Canada.

1959–1961 Resigned from CMHC and joined her husband in Jamaica, where he had gone

"My architectural training has enriched my life immeasurably. I cannot claim that any of these years has been dull."

HOUSING DESIGN PART I: plan of Churchill Park Village residential development showing single houses, townhouses and apartments focused upon a central community square. A. E. Searles and P. Meschino, planning consultants and architects.

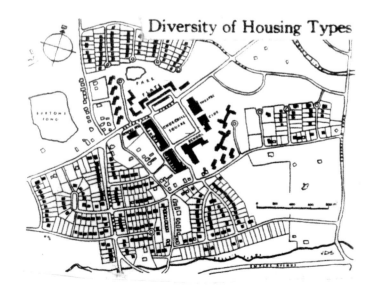

Diversity of Housing Types

to write features and train staff for the Jamaica Broadcasting Corporation. Worked as volunteer assistant and researcher for two years.

1962–1965 Two trips to the Yucatan peninsula researching the Mayans for a television special led to the decision to live in Mexico. The Stranges bought a house north of Chapala, in the state of Jalisco.

1983 Death of William Strange.

2002 on Jean Strange continues to live in Mexico, where she has taught Spanish to newcomers.

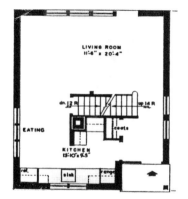
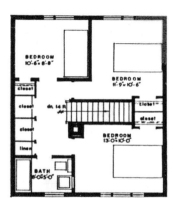

(TOP) CLASSIFICATION OF APARTMENT HOUSE DESIGNS: Allandale Apartments, Churchill Park Village, St. John's, Newfoundland, 1949, A.E. Searles and P. Meschino, Architects.

(BELOW) JEAN STRANGE AND ARCHITECT TED RAINES arranging an exhibit at the Design Centre, Elgin Street, Ottawa, 1954.

(ABOVE) SMALL HOUSE DESIGNS: floor plans and perspective of Design 507, Michael Bach, Architect.

JOAN ROBINSON GRIERSON

B.Arch. 1948, M.Sc. (Product Design) 1950

1948 B.Arch., University of Toronto.
1948–1950 Studied at the Chicago Institute of Design. The National Design Council granted bursaries to five Canadian students for two years' study of industrial and product design.
1950–1952 Assisted University of Toronto architecture professor Eric Arthur in research and preparation for the first National Gallery of Canada competition.
1952–1954 Worked at Page and Steele, Architects, Toronto: research for homes for the aged and interior design and furnishing specifications for the Ontario School for the Blind, Brantford, Ontario.
1954 Registered, Ontario Association of Architects. Travelled in Europe and Scandinavia. Worked at Sir Thomas Bennett and Sons, Architects, in London, UK; work included design of gas stations.

1955–1957 Worked at J. & J. Brook Limited, Contract Furnishing, of Montreal as a consultant on interior design.
1957 Married architect William Grierson in Toronto. Transferred to the Toronto office of J. & J. Brook Limited.
1958–1960 Two children born.
1960–2000 Independent architectural work: renovations and additions. Member of "For the Record," exhibit committee, 1986.
2001 William Grierson died.
2006 Continues with architectural practice on a smaller scale, and with editorial work on *For the Record.*

"This in-the-house-part-time practice has continued for over forty years. Projects have ranged in size from kitchens to buildings, but all work has been residential – no assignment was too large to be handled by a one-person office. This would have been much more difficult without the help and resources of my husband's office. Financial rewards are minimal and time and energy required considerable; however, the pleasure and satisfaction make it worthwhile."

(OPPOSITE AND BELOW) RENOVATIONS AND ADDITIONS TO THE HARRIS RESIDENCE, Barrie, Ontario, 1968. The farmhouse, divided into apartments, was restored to a single-family dwelling. A garage and a two-storey addition to the house were added and the interior renovated throughout. (From left) kitchen; first floor plan; second floor plan; exterior.

(ABOVE) DUPLEX BUNGALOW ON HILLSIDE SITE, Duntroon, Ontario, 1988, was altered and enlarged to provide two five-bedroom dwellings with communal areas. Original building (inset) and the enlarged building: a two-storey residence at either end and a communal area in the middle.

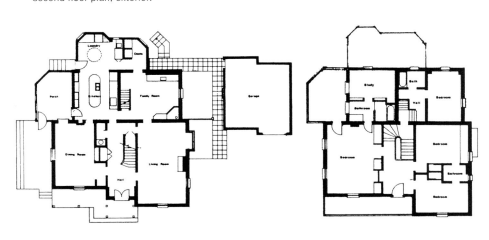

RUTHETTA KAPLAN REISS

B.Arch. 1949

1949 B.Arch., University of Toronto. Employed by office of Kaplan and Sprachman, Architects, Toronto. Married psychiatrist Harry Reiss.

1949–1950 Worked at the office of Rolf Dreyer, AIA, Poughkeepsie, New York.

1950–1953 Worked at the office of John Huntington, AIA, Hartford, Connecticut.

1954–1970 Raised two children.

1971–1975 Worked at the office of Kaneji Domoto, AIA, New Rochelle, New York.

1974–1977 Studied at the New York Botanical Gardens. Horticulture and landscape architecture certificate.

1978–1979 Worked at the office of Armand Benedek: landscape design for housing projects and the U.S. Air Force Academy in Denver, Colorado.

1979–89 Established Reiss-Ziegler Associates Inc. with Catherine Ziegler, a horticulturist, in Scarsdale, New York. Practice included landscape design for houses and small corporations. Taught landscape design at the New York Botanical Gardens, part-time, 1980–83.

1989 Reiss-Ziegler partnership was dissolved. Independent work: Design and supervision of apartment renovations in New York, landscape designs for synagogue extension and residential gardens.

1990–1997 Landscape work and architectural projects continued for some years.

2002 on Retirement.

"I would not advise anyone to study architecture who did not have talent and a great desire to use it. It is important not to be lured by the glamour of building: there is a lot of hard work and drudgery, and many projects remain in the drawers. There is also a lot of compromise when trying to balance your ideas, the client's ideas and the limitation of the budget.

"Still, I look forward to each new project and enjoy working out the problems. In most cases, I am happy with the results. Landscaping always improves with time, and it is a delight to visit former clients in the spring."

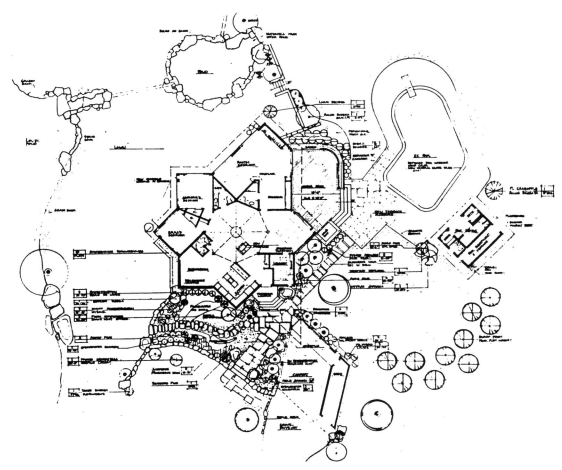

(ABOVE AND RIGHT) PRIVATE RESIDENCE, ARMONK, N.Y., 1986. This residence was originally designed in the 1940s by a follower of Frank Lloyd Wright. New garden plan and view of pool.

(OPPOSITE) LANDSCAPE DESIGN, Reiss-Ziegler Associates Inc., Private Residence, Stamford, Connecticut, 1980, view of garden pond.

THE 1950s

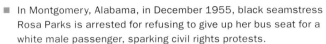

EVENTS

- Communist North Korea invades South Korea on June 25, 1950. Under UN command, troops from Britain, Australia, New Zealand and the United States are dispatched. The war ends in 1953.
- In Britain, the coronation of Elizabeth II is held on June 2, 1953.
- Joseph Stalin dies in Moscow in early 1953.
- Construction of a Distant Early Warning radar defence net is begun in early 1954 across northern Canada to protect North Americans from the perceived threat of Soviet missile attacks.
- In the fall of 1956, Soviet tanks crush a revolt in Hungary.
- John Diefenbaker elected prime minister in 1957.
- The Soviets launch Sputnik I into space on October 4, 1957.
- In the spring of 1959 the St. Lawrence Seaway opens, connecting shipping on the Great Lakes with the Atlantic.
- The Canadian government removes a federal ban on the hiring of married women.

LIFE

Rock and roll is everywhere. CBC TV is established, and television sets turn up in more and more homes. Radio stars such as Jack Benny, Frank Sinatra and Wayne & Shuster make the shift with ease. Canada Council for the Arts is created in 1957. The baby boom reaches its height.

- In Montgomery, Alabama, in December 1955, black seamstress Rosa Parks is arrested for refusing to give up her bus seat for a white male passenger, sparking civil rights protests.
- At sixteen, Marilyn Bell swims across Lake Ontario in 21 hours.
- In 1957, Prime Minister John Diefenbaker names Ellen Fairclough his government's secretary of state, making her Canada's first woman cabinet minister.

(LEFT) 1956 V-8 CHEVROLET with a wraparound windshield. **(TOP) DIAMOND CHAIR** by Harry Bertoia (1952), manufactured by the Knoll furniture company.

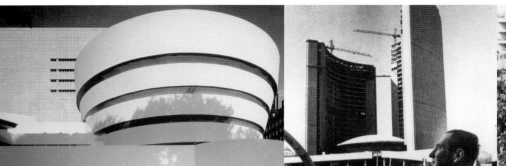

(LEFT TO RIGHT) GUGGENHEIM MUSEUM, New York, 1959, Frank Lloyd Wright, Architect; **TORONTO CITY HALL**, Toronto, 1957, Viljo Revell, Architect, Finland, built 1957 to 1964, in association with John B. Parkin Associates, Toronto; **CHANDIGHAR HOUSING**, India, 1956, Jane Drew, Architect.

STATISTICS
1951 POPULATION OF CANADA 14,009,400 Population of the U.S. 150,520,198
According to Statistics Canada, of 1,740 registered architects in Canada, 43 are women
Architecture graduates in Canada **37 WOMEN** 974 men

BOOKS *The Apprenticeship of Duddy Kravitz* by Mordecai Richler; *La Belle Bête* by Marie-Claire Blais; *Catcher in the Rye* by J.D. Salinger.
FILMS *Neighbours*, an Oscar-winning NFB film by Norman McLaren; *The African Queen*, directed by John Huston.
TELEVISION *Hockey Night in Canada*; *Don Messer's Jubilee*; *The Ed Sullivan Show*; *Gunsmoke*.
MUSIC "Heartbreak Hotel," Elvis Presley; "Diana," Paul Anka.
THEATRE Stratford Shakespearean Festival established; National Ballet founded by Celia Franca.
ART Painters Eleven (including Jack Bush, Kazuo Nakamura and Harold Town) organized to promote abstract art.

ARCHITECTURE

Large-scale building projects were under way across the country. The St. Lawrence Seaway, the largest engineering project at that time, required the construction of canals and the flooding of more than 100 square miles, including ten villages, to permit ocean-going vessels to reach the port of Thunder Bay on Lake Superior. In Kitimat, B.C., construction was started on a new town of 14,000 people. Above the Arctic Circle, the town of Inuvik was planned and built by the federal government. The first post-war community developed by private enterprise in North America,

the town of Don Mills was built on a 2,000-acre site north of Toronto.

The United States became the centre of innovation, with architects such as Frank Lloyd Wright, Ludwig Mies van der Rohe, Walter Gropius, Louis Kahn and Eero Saarinen. Each pursued his own path, adapting reinforced concrete to new forms and uses, exploring structural systems to span vast spaces and reinterpreting the International Style. Frank Lloyd Wright, who had pleaded for a "curb on America's lust for ugliness," died at the age of 91 in 1959.

Buckminster Fuller, an American designer and visionary, patented the geodesic dome in 1954. Extremely lightweight and stable, these domes do not require standard foundations and can cover large areas.

In Toronto, an international competition for the design of a new City Hall drew more than 500 entries from 42 countries. The winning design was by Finnish architect Viljo Revell, known for his bold, expressionist style. Two office towers curve around the circular council chamber.

In Vancouver, Ron Thom and Arthur Erickson developed a regional style that was influenced by Japanese architecture and Frank Lloyd Wright's organic architecture.

During the 1950s, a total of 36 women graduated with a degree in architecture from the following schools: University of British Columbia, 2; University of Manitoba, 15; University of Toronto, 8; McGill University, 11. First-year enrolment at the University of Toronto was set at 60.

(LEFT TO RIGHT) **GEODESIC COW BARN**, Senneville, Quebec, 1953–1954. Jeffrey Lindsay of Montreal had studied with Buckminster Fuller; **B.C. ELECTRIC BUILDING**, Vancouver, 1955, Thompson Berwick Pratt, with Ron Thom, Architects; **DON MILLS**, Ontario, 1958, the first large planned community in Canada.

LENNOX GRAFTON

B.Arch. 1950

1938–1941 Studied Household Economics, University of Alberta.

1942–1945 Weather observer in the RCAF, stationed at Hagersville, Ontario.

1950 B.Arch., University of Toronto.

1950–1951 Worked at Kaplan and Sprachman, Architects, Toronto. Registered, Ontario Association of Architects.

1951–1953 Worked at the Department of Defence in Ottawa on the reconstruction of RCAF bases.

1953–1955 Travelled in England for three months. Upon return to Canada, worked in architectural offices in Victoria and Prince George, British Columbia, and in Edmonton. Registered, Alberta Association of Architects.

1955–1956 Worked at the Department of Transport, Ottawa, building department.

1956–1960 Worked at Balharrie, Helmer and Morin, Architects, Pembroke, Ontario: residential and commercial buildings, schools and churches.

1960–1963 Established independent architectural practice in Arnprior, Ontario: work included McNab Township offices, church hall, school for March Township, residential design.

1963–1967 Taught secondary school home economics in Arnprior, Ontario, when loan to enlarge practice was refused.

1967 Joined the Ontario office of Public Works Canada in Toronto.

1969–1974 Design manager for Public Works Canada: Small Post Offices Program, First Nations schools and residences, RCMP renovations.

"Arnprior was in a prosperous area and the centre for a number of smaller towns – that is why I chose to work there. After being in practice for a while, I realized that larger jobs would go elsewhere unless I could enlarge the office. At that time, however, I was unable to borrow the money to do so from the bank. The supply of small jobs was diminishing and so I closed the office. Nonetheless, the whole thing has been very exciting. My work with the government was particularly interesting and demanding, and it required a lot of flexibility, energy and imagination."

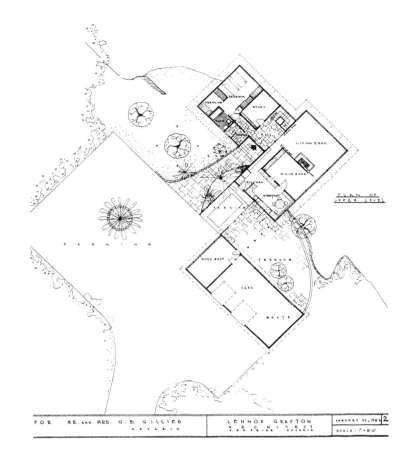

1974–1983 Project manager for Public Works Canada: Great Lakes Forest Research Centre at Sault Ste. Marie, Ontario; research laboratories for Energy, Mines and Resources at Elliot Lake, Ontario; Automatic Weather Stations for Agriculture Canada across Ontario and Western Canada; Marine Emergency Duties schools for Coast Guard Canada; housing and heating plant, Moose Factory, Ontario, for Health and Welfare Canada.
1983 Retired.
1986 "For the Record" exhibit research.
1990–2006 On the editorial board of *For the Record*.

GILLIES RESIDENCE, Braeside, Arnprior, Ontario, 1962. (Top) first floor plan; (right) south elevation.

(OPPOSITE) LENNOX GRAFTON, 1942, in her RCAF uniform.

LENNOX GRAFTON

1967–1974 DESIGN MANAGER
At Public Works Canada, a design manager is an architect or engineer in charge of the design aspects of a construction project. This involves the execution of the design itself, if that is not assigned to an independent firm, supervision of all plans and specifications and assistance to the project manager throughout the project.

ONTARIO MAP with locations of schools and other projects Lennox Grafton worked on as design manager and project manager for Public Works Canada.

(TOP) MARCH TOWNSHIP SCHOOL, Ontario, 1961–1962. Independent work.

(ABOVE) STAFF RESIDENCES with school in background, Attawapiskat, Public Works Canada; (below) floor plans of staff residences.

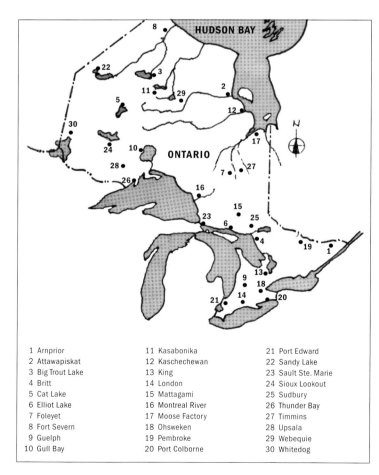

1 Arnprior	11 Kasabonika	21 Port Edward
2 Attawapiskat	12 Kaschechewan	22 Sandy Lake
3 Big Trout Lake	13 King	23 Sault Ste. Marie
4 Britt	14 London	24 Sioux Lookout
5 Cat Lake	15 Mattagami	25 Sudbury
6 Elliot Lake	16 Montreal River	26 Thunder Bay
7 Foleyet	17 Moose Factory	27 Timmins
8 Fort Severn	18 Ohsweken	28 Upsala
9 Guelph	19 Pembroke	29 Webequie
10 Gull Bay	20 Port Colborne	30 Whitedog

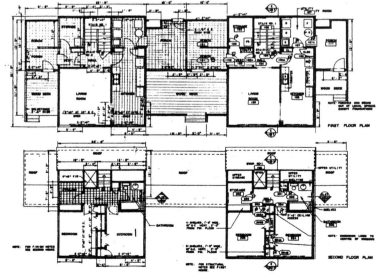

(LEFT)
ATTAWAPISKAT
SCHOOL, 1973–1976.
Aerial view of school
(airplane strut in
foreground).

(RIGHT)
KASCHECHEWAN
is one of seven
schools and resi-
dences designed for
the Ministry of Indian
and Northern Affairs
by Public Works
Canada; plan of
school.

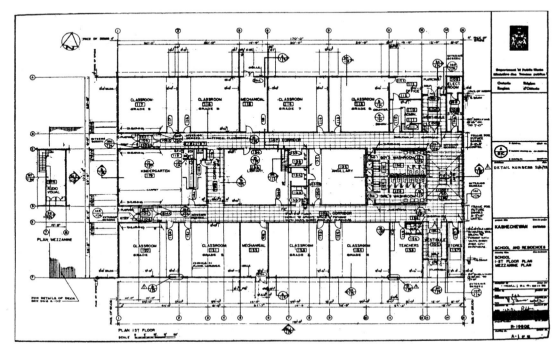

LENNOX GRAFTON

1974–1983 PROJECT MANAGER
The project manager is responsible for the administration of construction projects. This can involve site selection and land purchase for the client, scheduling of time and costs, coordination of construction and administration of the Crown's contracts with consultants and contractors.

(BELOW) 90-FOOT TOWER, AUTOMATIC WEATHER STATION, at Upsala, Ontario (90 miles west of Thunder Bay), 1981–1983.

(ABOVE) MARINE EMERGENCY DUTIES CENTRE, Canadian Coast Guard, Transport Canada, Port Colborne, Ontario, 1977–1980. Macdonald, Zuberec and Kamada Architects, St. Catharines, Ontario. On the Welland Canal, this school taught lifesaving skills to freshwater seamen, simulating emergency conditions at sea.

(BELOW) GREAT LAKES FOREST RESEARCH CENTRE, Sault Ste. Marie, Ontario, for Environment Canada, 1973–1976. William Burgoyne, Architect, Sault Ste. Marie, Ontario.

CATHERINE CURRIE SMALE

B.Arch. 1950

1950 B.Arch., University of Toronto.
1950–1952 Worked in the office of John Lang, Architect, Toronto.
1952 Married architect Warren Smale.
1952–1956 Worked at D.N. McIntosh, Architects and Engineers, Simcoe, Ontario: building design, working drawings, client negotiations.
1956–1965 Three children born.
1965 Registered, Ontario Association of Architects. Initiated an inventory of existing historical buildings in Norfolk County and participated in historical building conservation.
1966 President, University Women's Club, Norfolk County.
1968–1970 Worked in the office of Warren Smale, Architect, Simcoe, Ontario.
1970 Death of Warren Smale.
1971–1973 Initiated the recycling of the Duncan Campbell house, c. 1851, for use as Lynnwood Arts Centre, Simcoe, Ontario.

1972–1976 Involved in town and regional politics: first woman councillor, Town of Simcoe, Ontario; first chair, planning and development committee, Region of Haldimand/Norfolk.
1975 Acquired the Van Norman/Guiler House, built in 1840, and restored it; now designated under the Ontario Heritage Act.
1975–1984 Involved in Ontario and Canadian conservation: member, board of directors, Ontario Heritage Foundation; member, board of governors, Heritage Canada Foundation.
1979–1989 Consultant with C.A. Ventin, Architects Ltd., Simcoe Ontario, for historic building restoration and recycling.
1991 Catherine Smale died at the age of sixty-four in Simcoe, Ontario.

"My school career was quite undistinguished, but what I saw and learned and the people I studied and was associated with shaped my life. Young women of today seem to have achieved a sense of self-confidence which few of their female predecessors experienced until a later age. I think this is exciting – and good for the profession of architecture."

UNIVERSITY OF TORONTO CONVOCATION,
June 1950; (left to right) Lennox Grafton (B.Arch.), Catherine Currie (B.Arch.) and her sister, Marion Currie (B.Eng.).

CATHERINE CURRIE SMALE

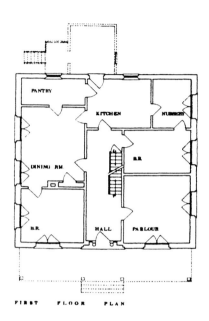

FIRST FLOOR PLAN

(ABOVE) 1978–1985 RESTORATION OF REGENCY COTTAGE, built by Romaine Van Norman in 1840; (left) first floor plan.

(BELOW) COUNTY OF HALTON COURTHOUSE AND JAIL, converted to a new town hall for Milton, Ontario 1984–1985. Interior design and furnishings by Catherine Smale.

MARGARET GISBORNE CHRISTIE

B.Arch. 1951

1940 After high school in Toronto, Margaret Gisborne planned to enroll in architecture, but the war intervened.

1940–1941 One-year course in business at Northern Vocational School.

1941–1942 Worked in an insurance office in Toronto.

1942–1946 Enlisted in the Women's Royal Canadian Naval Service, working in operations and signals. Discharged in 1946.

1946 Enrolled in the School of Architecture, University of Toronto. It was a record first year with one hundred students; ninety-four were veterans.

1951 B.Arch., University of Toronto.

1951–1952 Worked in the office of Marani and Morris, Architects: residential design and working drawings.

1952 Married James Christie, an architect and classmate, and moved to Stoney Creek, Ontario. Registered, Ontario Association of Architects.

1953–1977 Four children born. Part-time work in husband's office.

1977 on Member of the volunteer committee, chair of the building committee and member of the board of directors, Art Gallery of Hamilton. Peg Christie continued to work as a researcher and consultant in her husband's office.

2003 James Christie retired and the office closed.

2006 Continues to live in Stoney Creek.

Just after the war, the students at the School of Architecture invited Frank Lloyd Wright to visit the school and to lecture. As the secretary of the Architectural Society of the school, Peg Christie was involved with the arrangements. At the dinner, organized by the students, she remembers being escorted into the Toronto Club dining room on the arm of Frank Lloyd Wright.

MARGARET GISBORNE CHRISTIE

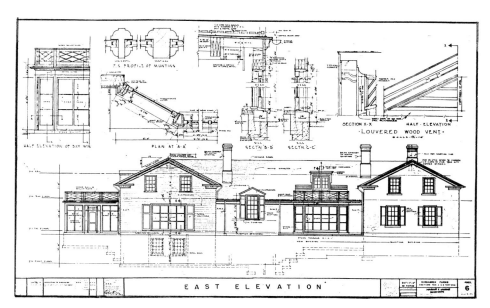

(TOP) KINGHAVEN FARMS ADDITION, 1952; west elevation and first and second floor plans. Marani and Morris, Architects, Toronto, Ontario.

(LEFT) SAMPLE OF A WORKING DRAWING, showing east elevation and details,

MARJORIE SEWELL SHEPLAND

B.Arch. 1953

1953 B.Arch., University of Toronto.
1953–1955 Employed by office of James William Kideney, Architect, Buffalo, New York: working drawings for public housing, office buildings, schools and libraries.
1955 Married architect Ronald E. Shepland.
1955–1957 Employed by office of Arthur Jenkins, Architect, Fayetteville, North Carolina: working drawings, mostly for schools.
1957–1960 Employed by office of C. Storrs Barrows, Architect, Rochester, New York: working drawings for libraries, houses, schools.

1960–1971 Raised three children.
1971–1991 Worked (part-time) at Shepland Partnership Architects (Ronald E. Shepland and Tsukasa Hatakeyama), Rochester, New York. Involved in various aspects of practice, from working drawings and interiors to accounting. Projects included schools, health-care facilities, libraries, industrial and commercial buildings.
1992 Eased into retirement with the construction of the Shepland home, designed with her husband, in Biltmore Forest, North Carolina.
2006 Enjoys travel and ink sketching.

"By the time I was twelve, I had determined that architecture was to be my field of endeavor. Although my family always held priority over my career, part-time work in one's chosen occupation provides great satisfaction. Never did I regret my choice of profession, and marrying an architect helps!"

SHEPLAND HOUSE, Biltmore Forest, North Carolina, 1992.

AUDREY KOEHLER CHRISTIE

B.Arch. 1954

1954–1958 B.Arch., Honours, University of Toronto. Award: Toronto Brick Prize (third year). Married Robert Christie, geologist. Worked part-time at the office of Henry Fliess, Architect, on housing. Two children born. Independent work: two houses.

1958–1962 Moved to Ottawa. Worked at Central Mortgage and Housing Corporation, architectural and planning department. Registered, Ontario Association of Architects. Travelled in Europe with children, 1960. Birth of third child.

1962–1968 Contract work with Edward Cuhaci, Architect: offices, apartments, houses, schools, northern hostels. Competitions with E. Cuhaci, W. Lewandowski and M. Pine Architects. Art teacher, children's classes, Ottawa Municipal Art Centre. Adoption of fourth child and birth of fifth.

Independent work: house, cottages, renovations and additions.

1968–1974 Moved to Calgary. Raised five children. Six months' residence with family in Grise Fjord, a small Inuit community in the Northwest Territories; taught children's art classes. In Calgary, was a founder of the Saturday School, an alternative elementary school based on the arts; taught art and mathematics. Worked with Don Snow, Architect, Calgary: two preliminary school designs.

1974 Christie family went on a geological exchange to Copenhagen, Denmark, for one year.

1975–1988 In Calgary, worked for T. Laird, Colin Bell and D.M. Snow, Architects: renovations, offices, houses, senior citizens' apartments, recreation complex, church, design for proposed multi-use arts centre

"In many ways, architecture is the perfect profession for a woman because of the flexibility it offers to fit a practice around family events and daily responsibilities. These very facts produce their own problems, of course, and distractions are always close at hand.

"My life as an architect could never be compared to that of someone with her own office and established practice. This was not possible. However, I have been able to practice independently as an architect, with the assistance of help at home, and I feel very satisfied with the opportunities that have come my way."

for the North Peace Arts Council. Member of Co-Design Calgary, a team of artists and architects, translating verbal ideas of community groups into sketches for use in project proposals. Work with Society for Preservation of Architectural Resources in Calgary: preparation of proposals for appropriate use of heritage properties, including a joint project with the University of Calgary Urban Lab – proposing an urban studies centre and city museum for Calgary's No. 1 fire hall. Independent work: house renovations and additions, design and construction supervision of family residence, prototype inner-city house with passive solar-attic assist to the heating system, design and construction of second solar-attic house.

1988–2000 Worked at D.M. Snow, Architect, Calgary: design and preliminary drawings for St. Peter's Anglican Church, Okotoks, Alberta. Independent work: interior design for miniatures shop in Oshawa, Ontario; renovation and restoration schemes for 1841 stone farmhouse, Ivanhoe, Ontario.
2001 Death of Robert Christie.
2002 Moved to Denman Island, B.C.
2004 Audrey Christie died in Courtenay, B.C.

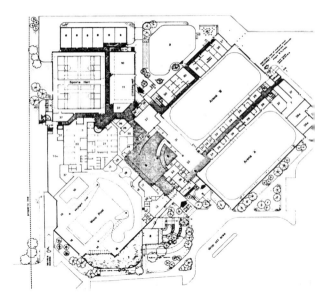

RECREATIONAL COMPLEX FOR THE CITY OF CALGARY. (Above) view of main entrance; (below) first floor plan. Work with Don M. Snow, Architect: Southland Leisure Centre. The scheme was submitted to the City of Calgary by Camrec Facilities, Edmonton 1979. Audrey Christie was designer and associate project manager.

CONTRACT DESIGN WITH EDWARD CUHACI, ARCHITECT, OTTAWA, ONTARIO. Dustbane Products Building, Ottawa, Ontario, 1962.

AUDREY KOEHLER CHRISTIE

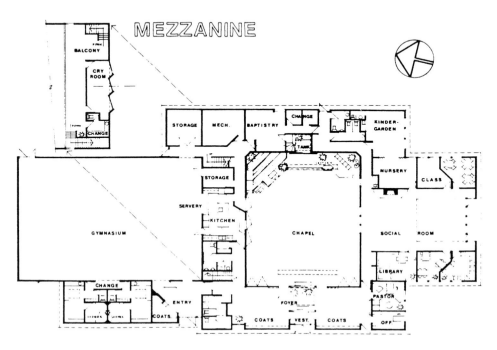

RANCHLANDS COMMMUNITY CHURCH,
Reorganized Church of the Latter Day Saints,
Calgary, Alberta, 1982. Work with D.M. Snow,
Architect: design drawings and construction
supervision by Audrey Christie. (Above) interior
views; (above, left) plan; (left) exterior view.

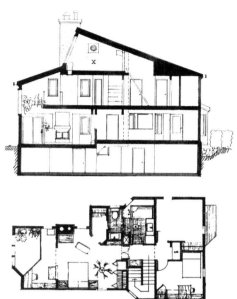

CHRISTIE RESIDENCE, Calgary, Alberta, 1982. Solar attic provides heat. **(RIGHT, TOP TO BOTTOM)** Section showing solar attic; first and second floor plans; (left) living room.

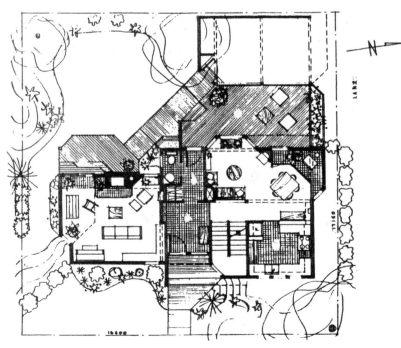

JOAN BURT

B.Arch. 1956

1956 B.Arch., University of Toronto.
1956–1958 Worked at Mathers & Haldenby, Architects, Toronto.
1958–1959 Worked with developer Irwin Burns of Burcon Construction.
1958 Registered, Ontario Association of Architects. Established independent office and practice in Toronto.
1958 on At the beginning, the practice focused on the restoration of downtown Toronto districts and buildings. This included identifying architecturally significant buildings to restore and renovate, matching client to building, project and marketing. In later years, the work expanded into southern Ontario, with more new construction, as well as interior and landscape design. The practice revitalized architecturally significant areas: Belmont Street, Cabbagetown, King and Berkeley, King and Jarvis, King and Wilkins; similar work in Niagara-on-the-Lake and Collingwood. Member of the Canadian Association of Professional Heritage Consultants.

CONCURRENT WITH THE ARCHITECTURAL PRACTICE:
1964–1970 Owned antique store, specializing in furniture and artifacts.
1965 Ontario College of Art: joined the Faculty of Interior Design.
1970–1985 Ontario College of Art: developed and chaired the Department of Design (environmental design, ceramics, textiles, glass and multimedia print).

"In the early years of my practice there were limited opportunities for women, so I invented projects and found developers to facilitate the work. I focused on rowhouses, and was eventually credited with initiating the redevelopment of the Cabbagetown neighbourhood in Toronto.

"The livability of our cities depends upon the preservation and enhancement of the streetscape. This core belief led to my interest in the restoration and re-use of historic buildings. As the practice developed, it became apparent that to create a more fully developed environment, interior design, landscape design and the decorative arts needed to be integrated into the architectural work. This relationship allowed for the dynamic development of new ideas and realities."

AWARDS

Beautify Toronto Award for work to buildings on Berkeley Street between King and Adelaide and 300 King Street East. The Niagara-on-the-Lake Historical Society recognition for relocating and reconstructing an 1840 Port Hope farmhouse to 115 Ricardo Street, Niagara-on-the-Lake. Plaques for Heritage Buildings, Toronto Historical Board, City of Toronto Sesquicentennial, including homes on Belmont Street and Alpha Avenue.

ROWHOUSES, 4–26 Belmont Street, Toronto, 1965. Development and design. (Top left) rear elevation and bedroom terrace; (top right) street view; (left) sketch of front elevation showing cast-iron fence and planting.

(BELOW) NIENKAMPER SHOWROOM BUILDING, 300 King Street East, Toronto, 1970. Design and construction. (Below left) King Street elevation; (below, from top) open stairs to second floor; showroom at entry.

JOAN BURT

(RIGHT) DAVIS HOUSE, Oakville, 1997. Front elevation of the new "historic" house.

(BELOW) DAYMOND HOUSE, Guelph, 1991. Architectural design, interior design and landscape design. (Below right) front elevation; (below, from top) living room from bridge above; dining room.

O'REILLY RESIDENCE, Etobicoke, 1999. Architectural design, interior design and landscape design. (Left) front elevation; (right) rear elevation and garden.

RENNIE GUEST POOL HOUSE, part of a vineyard estate in progress, Beamsville Bench, Ontario, 2003. (Left) lakeside elevation; (right) view from ponds.

JOANNA BARCLAY DE TOLLY OZDOWSKI

Dip. Eng. Arch. 1949, B.Arch. 1957

1945 Fled from Poland to Germany.
1949 Married Jan Ozdowski, civil engineer, in Munich. Diploma, Engineering and Architecture, Department of Engineering, University of Munich.
1950–1955 Emigrated to Canada with husband. Worked in architectural offices in Toronto: James Haffa, 1950; Gibson and Pokorny, 1950–1952; Sproatt and Rolph, 1952–1955.
1955 Enrolled in fourth year, School of Architecture, University of Toronto.
1957 B.Arch., University of Toronto. Registered, Ontario Association of Architects. Worked in the office of Sproatt and Rolph, Architects.

1962–1991 Established independent practice in Toronto. Architectural work included religious, commercial, residential and industrial buildings.
1964 Award from Central Mortgage and Housing Corporation for housing design.
1992 Retired.
2006 Living in Copernicus Lodge.

"Professional status was not easy to get. After two years of architectural work, the admissions council of the Ontario Association of Architects said, 'Back to school for two years.' Harsh as it seemed at the time, it was the right decision.

"Both my husband and I have benefited from our architectural/structural association. His experience has been a great strength to me, and his help was always there. I always enjoyed my work, no matter how difficult it became. In my practice, I tried not to lose sight of the purpose, which is closer to art than money. The excellence of the finished work was a source of satisfaction to me."

CRAWFORD HOUSE, Kingsway Crescent, Toronto, 1962. Canadian Housing Design Council Award 1964. (Left) front entrance, (below left) rear view.

(ABOVE) BOSLEY HOUSE, Old George Place, Toronto, 1966.

JOANNA BARCLAY DE TOLLY OZDOWSKI

ST. HEDWIG'S CHURCH, Oshawa, Ontario, 1958. Inadequate size of phase I basement resulted in cantilevered aisles. (Left) stained glass windows at altar wall; (right) entrance of church.

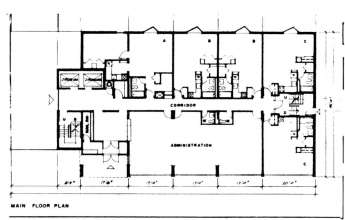

MAIN FLOOR PLAN

COPERNICUS LODGE for senior citizens, Toronto, 1977. Part one of two-part building program. Projecting L-shaped windows allow views of the lake and the city. (Left) view of Lodge from street; (right) plan of main floor.

(RIGHT) CONVENT ADDITION for the Felician Sisters, Mississauga, Ontario, 1981. New living quarters were added to the existing convent, an old house on a treed site. (Clockwise from top left) second floor plan and room layout; interior of the chapel from balcony; south side of the building: the chapel is on the far right.

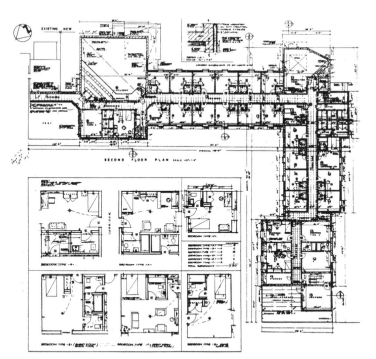

(LEFT) SILVANO COLOR LABORATORIES, Toronto, Ontario, 1979.

KATHLEEN CONNOR IRVINE

B.Arch. 1958

1958 B.Arch., University of Toronto.
1959 Worked at Balharrie, Helmer and Morin, Architects, Ottawa.
1960 Worked at Peter Dickinson, Architect, Montreal.
1961 Married Brian Irvine, educator.
1961–1963 Worked at Bemi and Murray, Architects, Ottawa.
1963–1979 Raised three children. Independent work: family cottage (1971), two residences (1976, 1978).
1979–1982 Volunteer work: coordinated design for a local playground. Taught ceramics at night school. Tour guide and member of the committee for costumes and quilt making at Billings Estate, an 1828 house belonging to the City of Ottawa.
1981–1985 Worked at Murray and Murray, Griffiths and Rankin, Architects, Ottawa.

Kanata Town Centre – job captain for the working drawings of a six-theatre Cineplex; Place d'Orléans Shopping Mall; Ottawa International Airport; with a team of twelve, worked on additions and renovations. Natural Resources College, Lilongwe, Malawi, built by the Canadian International Development Agency (CIDA). Stornoway, Ottawa, residence of the Leader of the Opposition: renovations.
1986–1988 Worked at the office of Murray and Murray, Architects, Ottawa. Minto Suite Hotel and office complex – member of team developing working drawings for hotel units, office towers and two floors of shops. Place Bell Canada, coordinated the design with the client, consultants and architects for two floors of executive offices.
1988–1989 Worked at the office of Anthony

"During the years with small children, I did not feel it would be to my benefit to pay an annual professional fee. Then as time went by, the professional entrance requirements became so demanding that I hesitated and questioned the expense.

"To a woman today, interested in architecture, I would like to say that maintaining a career may be as challenging now as it was in the fifties. If your abilities indicate architecture, then go to it – and good luck!"

Pearson, Architect, Ottawa. Energy, Mines and Resources: coordinator for two new floor layouts. Ottawa residence, design, renovations and working drawings.

1989 Retired.

2006 Enjoying volunteer work and travel.

BRATHWAITE HOUSE,
Ottawa, Ontario, 1978.

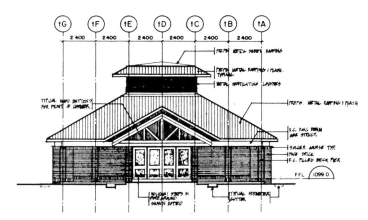

NATURAL RESOURCES COLLEGE, Lilongwe, Malawi, 1984, CIDA project manager. (Right) working drawings for lecture theatre; (above) view of the campus.

MARY PATTERSON CLARK

B.Arch. 1959, M.Sc. (planning) 1984

1959 B.Arch., University of Toronto. Married fellow architectural graduate Clive Clark.
1959–1960 Worked at Weir and Cripps, Architects, North Bay, Ontario.
1960–1962 Toured Europe. Lived in Copenhagen (Clive Clark worked in the office of Arne Jacobsen, Architect). Co-author of report to Ontario government on Swedish civil defence shelter construction. Birth of a son. Worked part-time at Irving Grossman, Architect, Toronto.
1962–1972 Raised family, now including two daughters. Independent work: additions and renovations.
1972 Worked at James Weller, Architect, Toronto: research coordinator for Rouge Industrial Land Use Study. This led to work in urban planning.
1973 Registered, OAA. Returning to an archi-

tectural office was under consideration when a job offer in land-use planning led into the transportation planning field.
1973–1975 Metro Toronto Transportation Plan Review: evaluation of development potential associated with transportation options to the year 2000.
1976 Metro Toronto Planning Department (Transportation Division): Light Rail Transit feasibility studies for Scarborough, Ontario.
1977–1979 Urban Transportation Development Corporation: coordinator of urban design study to explore the potential of elevated rapid transit in urban and suburban environments.
1979–1980 Volunteer with Vietnamese "Boat People."
1980–1981 Worked at Barton Myers Associates, Architects, Toronto: urban integration

"Entering architectural studies opened up a whole world of interest and challenge. I developed a totally new perception of the world. I've always been impressed with the multilevel interest of architects in design.

"It seemed to me that small-scale design projects combined with child-raising held the potential for a very satisfying life. However, the design of low-budget renovations and additions is difficult under the best conditions. As my clientele extended beyond personal contacts, I found it difficult to emerge from projects feeling my approach to design was completely satisfied."

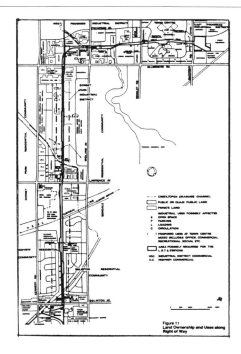

Figure 11
Land Ownership and Uses along
Right of Way

analysis, rapid transit project, Hamilton, Ontario.

1982–1984 Graduate studies in urban planning: M.Sc. (planning), University of Toronto.

1985–1997 "For the Record" exhibit committee and archival research. Independent architectural and planning work.

1986–2000 Worked with Comarc Architects, Nunavut, commercial and residential.

1994–2000 Life divided between Toronto and Nunavut (husband's practice was in Iqaluit). Documentation of historical development of Iqaluit.

2000 Retired.

2002 Geomatics Canada, Iqaluit Development Mapping, historical input. Summers are spent in the Arctic.

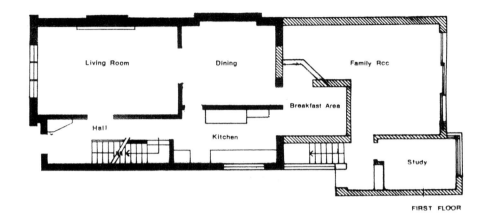

FIRST FLOOR

CRATH HOUSE ADDITION, Toronto, 1972. (Above) plan of first floor – addition shown hatched; (below, left) interior view toward dining room; (below, right) garden view of house.

(OPPOSITE) SCARBOROUGH LIGHT RAIL TRANSIT Feasibility Study, 1977. For the Metropolitan Toronto Planning Department. Mary Clark identified the role of the transit line in the development of Scarborough, participated in route evaluations, and was responsible for the basic layout and graphic design of the report (excerpt shown here).

MONICA NOMBERG

B.Arch. 1959

1950 Left Poland with her family and travelled to Israel.

1951 Emigrated to Winnipeg.

1954 Enrolled in the School of Architecture, University of Manitoba.

1955 Family moved to Toronto; Nomberg enrolled in second year, School of Architecture, University of Toronto.

1959 B.Arch., University of Toronto.

1959–1960 Worked at Lipson and Daskin, Architects, Toronto.

1960–1965 Worked at Edward Durrell Stone, Architect, New York, as a junior designer.

1965–1966 Moved to London, England. Worked at the Ministry of Housing and Local Government: town planning applied to computer program development.

1966–1968 Worked in London with her husband, who was a professional photographer.

1968 Returned to the firm of Edward Durrell Stone in New York. (When Edward Durrell Stone retired in 1975, the firm became Edward Durrell Stone Associates.)

1975 Project architect in charge of design, Edward Durell Stone Associates.

1982 Vice-president of the firm.

1994–1995 Stone Associates undertook master plan and architectural design of Staten Island Community College. Monica Nomberg was responsible for the design of the performing arts building, which included a theatre and art gallery.

1995–1996 Stone Associates office closed. Monica Nomberg and a colleague pursued independent work.

1997 Retired.

2006 Living in New York and travelling.

"You get tired of being different – which is to say, being a woman – and tired of fighting the battle to prove yourself. At university, I had been given the same recognition as my male counterparts, but in the professional world it did not happen. However, this is changing. I have gained more self-assurance in my role, and the business world is more accepting of professional women."

(RIGHT) STATE UNIVERSITY OF NEW YORK AT ALBANY, 1962. Design concept of library (aerial view). Junior designer, detailing phases of the work and assisting in design development.

(LEFT) DICONIX HEADQUARTERS, with laboratories for research and development in computer technology, Dayton, Ohio, 1985. Project architect in charge of design. Member of the team during early design stages, responsible for client liaison, consultants and site visits.

MONICA NOMBERG

SINCLAIR COMMUNITY COLLEGE, Dayton, Ohio. Project began with a master plan in 1968. Stone Associates were the architects for all phases. Project architect for phases V, VI and VII. (Right) courtyard; (bottom) aerial view.

(LEFT) MUSEUM OF MODERN ART RESIDENTIAL TOWER, New York, 1985, Cesar Pelli, Architect and Edward Durrell Stone Associates, Associated Architects (design development) for the exterior, D. Stone Associates P.C., architects for the interior.

FINANCIAL SQUARE OFFICE BUILDING, New York, begun in 1986. Project architect on the last prime waterfront location in the financial district. (Bottom left) rendering superimposed on the waterfront skyline; (bottom right) rendering: view from corner of Old Slip and Front streets.

NATALIE SALKAUSKIS LIACAS

B.Arch. 1960

1949 Immigrated with family to Canada from Germany, having fled there from Lithuania in 1944.
1960 B.Arch., University of Toronto.
1960–1961 Worked at Gilleland and Janiss, Architects, Toronto.
1961 Married Walter Liacas, an architect.
1961–1963 Worked at Pentland and Baker, Architects.
1963 Registered, Ontario Association of Architects.
1963–1965 Worked at Eero Saarinen and Associates, Hamden, Connecticut. (Walter Liacas did postgraduate work at Yale during this time.)
1965–1967 Worked at Raymond Moriyama, Architect, Toronto.

1967–1969 Worked at Shore and Moffat, Architects, Toronto.
1969–1994 Worked for the Design Services Branch, Ministry of Government Services, Ontario.
1972, 1977 Two children.
1994–1996 Registered, private practice.
1996–2003 Vice-president and president of Canadian Council of Central and East European Communities. Executive vice-president, Lithuanian Canadian Community.
2000 on Planning and design consultant.

"The best part of being an architect is that I very much enjoy every moment that I work. The worst of it is that I have missed out on the art of living due to my overinvolvement and spartan attitudes. Except for household responsibilities, my energies are entirely channelled toward current projects. One should learn how to handle this situation from the very beginning. Nonetheless, it is one of the best professions a woman can have."

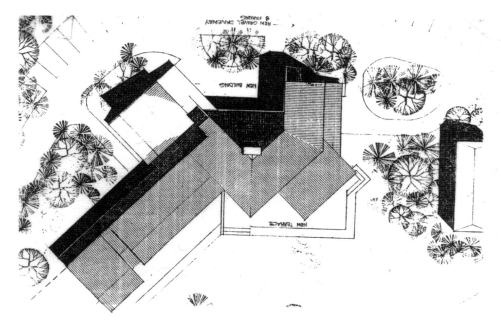

STAFF DEVELOPMENT CENTRE for the Ontario Public Service, Barrie, Ontario, 1970. (Left) roof plan; (above) exterior view.

ONTARIO CAMP LEADERSHIP CENTRE, Ministry of Education, Bark Lake, Haliburton, Ontario, 1972. (Left) exterior view and (above) perspective sketch.

(OPPOSITE) LIACAS AND COLLEAGUES AT SITE.

NATALIE SALKAUSKIS LIACAS

ONTARIO PAVILION, International Garden and Greenery Exposition (Expo '90), Osaka, Japan. Designed for the Ontario Ministry of Tourism as the province's entry, the garden won first prize. (Right) interior showing exhibit; (below) front exterior.

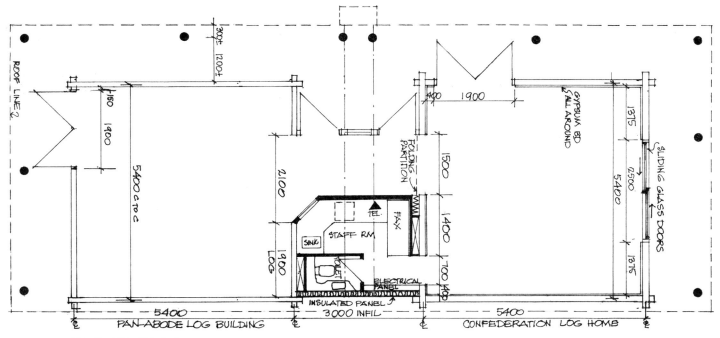

ROOF LINE 2

3000

1200

150

1900

5400 c to c

2100

1900

1900

SINK

STAFF RM

400

1900

1400

1500

FOLDING PARTITION

TEL.

FAX

ELECTRICAL PANEL

INSULATED PANEL
3000 INFIL

GYPSUM BD ALL AROUND

1375

2500

5400

1375

SLIDING GLASS DOORS

700

400

5400

PAN-ABODE LOG BUILDING

5400

CONFEDERATION LOG HOME

FLOOR PLAN   SCALE : 1:50

WEST ELEVATION

ONTARIO PAVILION,
Expo '90, Osaka,
Japan. (Above) floor
plans; (left) elevation
showing the log
building and deck.
These structures
were precut and
shipped to Japan
for assembly.

NATALIE SALKAUSKIS LIACAS

TRAVEL CENTRES for the Ontario Ministry of Tourism, 1992: (top left) Fort Frances, Rainy River District of northwestern Ontario; (top right) Hill Island, Thousand Islands; (right) Hawkesbury, eastern Ontario, near the border with Quebec. The design prototype was modified for different locations, united by a common visual identity.

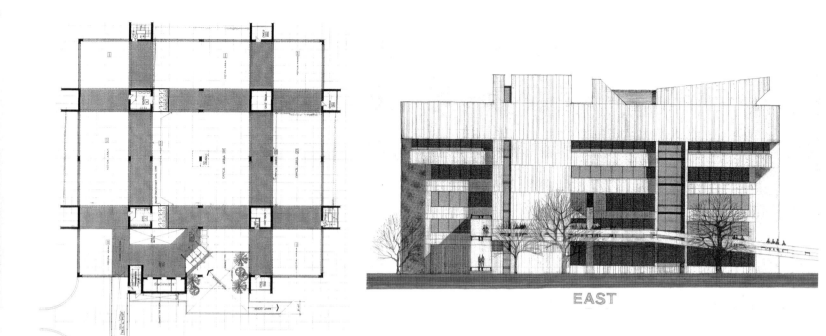

EAST

FEASIBILITY STUDIES: Addition to the Administration building for the Department of Highways, Downsview, Ontario, 1969, elevation and main floor plan.

OLD CITY HALL, Toronto, refurbishment study for the Ministry of Government Services, 1988, perspective of enclosed courtyard (drawing by Gordon Grice).

EPILOGUE

In 1986, the "For the Record" exhibit marked the centennial of the enrolment of women at the University of Toronto. The exhibit and its scrapbooks, now in the archives of the University of Toronto, offered a chance to study the background and abilities of these women graduates, the choices open to them, as well as the times in which they lived and practiced architecture.

Marjorie Hill was the first woman to graduate in architecture in Canada. Marjorie's mother had enrolled at the University of Toronto, when women were first accepted in 1884. She had been interested in architecture herself, but was told it was not "lady-like" and pursued it no further. Her father was a science teacher who became head of the Edmonton Library. With the full support of her parents, Marjorie enrolled in architecture at the University of Alberta after completing a B.A. degree. She had no knowledge of other women in the profession.

Jean Hall, who followed, felt an arts degree would not fit her for a profession. Her sister was a medical student, her father a builder and enthusiastic about Jean's choice of architecture. Jean had a talent for drawing and painting, and a "mechanical turn of mind."

Phyllis Cook had loved drawing and painting since she was a child. She was an unremarkable student in high school but was outstanding in architecture, graduating with several prizes and honours.

Many of the women demonstrated early abilities not only in drawing and painting but also aptitude for mathematics and physics. Four of them – Alice Ayer, Pegeen Synge, Joan Grierson and Audrey Christie – attended the children's art classes at the Art Gallery of Ontario. Audrey went on to Saturday morning classes with Arthur Lismer when in high school.

Making the choice was not always easy. Dama Bell was a qualified elementary school teacher when she entered architecture in 1929. Her father, a dental surgeon, objected strenuously; her mother paid her tuition, and Dama paid her living expenses from managing a local summer tourist camp, working in architectural offices and, in her final year, with the help of a loan.

Katharine Helm's grandfather was an architect, and her father was the artist C.W. Jefferys, who taught in the School of Architecture at the University of Toronto. However, medicine and archaeology were her first choices; as she said, it was lack of money that led her into architecture. Isobel Stewart chose architecture as it seemed preferable to struggling as an artist. Her high school principal was against it.

Audrey Christie tested high in math, mechanical and artistic skills. She was directed to home economics, while engineering was suggested to a fellow male student with the same test results. But Audrey had studied the calendar outlining the studies for architecture, and all attempts to dissuade her failed.

Joan Burt did well in math and sciences in high school. She then spent more than a year in Honours Science at the University of Toronto, considering her options, before settling on architecture. It was an interview with the director of the School of Architecture, Col. H.H Madill, that convinced her.

The families of these women architects were largely supportive. Ruthetta Reiss's father was a partner in an architectural firm. He believed women should be trained to support themselves. Alice Ayer's mother was a doctor, her father a science teacher. She felt her choice was between art college and medicine. When a fellow student in an art class suggested architecture, the pieces fell into place. (The student was Pegeen Synge.) Two of the graduates had sisters who studied medicine and electrical engineering.

The Great Depression may well have contributed to the drive felt by many women to be financially independent. There are glimpses of the times in their stories – the Great Depression, slow economic recovery, the war and the years that followed.

The Depression closed many architectural offices. *Fortune* magazine was exaggerating when it stated that during the Depression, one out of every two architects was out of work. It was almost true. Consequently, architecture students found it difficult to acquire the experience they needed to complete the degree. In 1929, Dama Bell had entered a class of eighteen at the University of Toronto. When nine finished five years later, none had the twelve months' experience required to graduate. Katharine Helm lacked nine months' experience one year later, and never did graduate.

After graduation, many found work in department stores in interior design and furnishings. Marjorie Hill spent a summer working at Eaton's College Street store, just blocks from the School of Architecture. Bea Davidson worked in a factory for a jewellery firm, and Dama Bell found work at Adam's Furniture Store. After graduating with Honours in 1935, Phyllis Cook spent two years at Eaton's.

Magazines and radio provided another source of income and opportunities for expression. Marjorie Hill wrote several articles on "Better Building" for *Agricultural Alberta* magazine in the two years following graduation. Betty Harding and Joan Burt's work appeared in *Canadian Homes and Gardens*. Audrey Christie wrote for *Ontario Homes and Living*. On the CBC radio, Phyllis Cook delivered weekly fifteen-minute talks on house renovation. Later, Pegeen Dryer was responsible for over fifty radio broadcasts, covering new house design and community planning.

Teaching was an alternative route for some. While waiting for registration, Marjorie Hill taught in a rural Alberta school. Jean Hall also taught in Alberta for two years when she was an architectural student. After the Second World War, Lennox Grafton taught household economics for four years in Arnprior, Ontario.

Just before the war, Ann Malott, to complete the practical experience for her degree, joined the staff of the Ontario Department of Public Works for a three-month trial period in 1937. Due to an outside complaint that the government had no right to hire a female when male architects were unemployed, she was let go. The chief draftsman was outraged and successfully argued for her reinstatement at a higher salary some time later. In New York, after the war had started, she found work in the architectural office of the Rockefeller Center – the first woman hired there. Her boss later admitted he had wanted to see the men's faces when a "skirt" walked into the office.

Jean Strange from Yorkshire, England, was touring Canada with students when war broke out. She entered second year at the University of Toronto School of Architecture. Susan Lovely, a British citizen who had been living in Japan and whose father had been imprisoned by the Japanese, spent two years studying architecture at the University of Toronto before returning to England.

The Second World War brought change to the role of women in society. The armed services accepted women. Margaret Gisborne and Jean Strange joined the WRCN, and Lennox Grafton joined the RCAF. Students who were married, such as Isabel Stewart and Shelagh Rounthwaite, adjusted their education to their husband's posting. University classes adjusted to the changing numbers. One man found himself in a class of three at the University of Toronto School of Architecture – with Pegeen Synge and Alice Ayer.

Summer work experience was affected. Joan Grierson found her first summer job at Wartime Housing. Mary Imrie spent her final summer as an architectural student (1943) at the Toronto Shipbuilding Company, which was manufacturing minesweepers for the British Navy. She did "collection and charting of production statistics" for four months. In 1944, Mary graduated and looked for work. The first architectural office refused to hire a woman, but she found another.

The end of the war brought together the largest group of first-year students that the School of Architecture had ever seen. There were 100 students in January 1946 – five of them were women. At the end of the five-year program, fifty-two men and two women graduated, Lennox Grafton and Catherine Smale. Margaret Gisborne followed the next year; she had joined the class of 1951, which included ninety-five returning servicemen. Class sizes were never reduced to the small numbers they had been before the war.

During the 1950s, the enrolment in first-year architecture was set at sixty, and by the time most of these classes graduated, there was only one woman in each. Among them were Joanna Ozdowski from Germany, Monica Nomberg from Poland, and Natalie Liacas, from Lithuania via Germany. One of their offspring described them as "boaters," referring to their arrival across the Atlantic from Europe. As architects they have led busy professional lives.

Others found their own niche. Joan Burt became a pioneer in the restoration of inner city neighbourhoods. Audrey Christie had no ambition to become a famous architect but did have a burning interest in all aspects of design. She went on to work as a design consultant with architectural firms in Ottawa and Calgary while raising five children.

The graduates of the 1950s found work more available to women. However, even in the postwar years, while waiting for an architectural job, Audrey Christie worked as a sales clerk at Simpson's department store and attended the store's Interior Design School, studying "Plain, Pattern and Stripe" rules of decoration. In 1956, Monica Nomberg worked at Eaton's.

The first twenty years were very difficult for those who graduated before the Second World War. They were climbing single file up a very steep slope. After the war, social acceptance of women in the work force increased and there was a building boom. This meant work for these women architects.

Eight chose independent practice, with an office in the home (Carlisle, Stewart, Alison, Dryer, Grierson, Smale, Clark). Four became sole practitioners (Ozdowski, Burt, Stewart, Hill). One operated as a consultant with established firms in Ottawa and Calgary (Audrey Christie). Imrie and Wallbridge established a firm in Edmonton; their practice lasted for twenty-eight years. Three found work with the government, which has always served women well (Grafton, Strange, Liacas).

Some pursued additional training. Bea Davidson completed a master's degree in architecture. Isobel Stewart took a three-month course at the Society for the Preservation of Ancient Buildings, in London, England. Alice Ayer Alison completed a degree in Preservation Architecture at Columbia University and was one of twenty founders of the Association for Preservation Technology in the Gaspé. Joan Grierson completed a master's degree in Product Design. Mary Clark did a master's in Urban Planning.

All these women have shared the sense that their education in architecture has led to a lifetime of experience.

DEVELOPMENTS IN PROFESSIONAL STANDARDS

By 1960, the total number of women who had graduated from Canadian schools of architecture was ninety-seven. At that time there were four universities offering an architectural program – Toronto, McGill, Manitoba and British Columbia. (The school of architecture at the University of Alberta had closed in 1939.) There are now eleven schools of architecture, and the enrolment of women has been rapidly increasing at such a rate that the number of women graduates in architecture is rapidly approaching that of men. The graph in Appendix C details the changes.

Education has evolved from a five-year B.Arch. course, including a year of practical experience, to a graduate course leading to an M.Arch. degree. Each school has its particular requirements and timetable (see Appendix D). With the M.Arch. in hand, most graduates choose to qualify for registration with a provincial association. To do this, they enter an internship program, which may take three to five or more years.

Graduate architects working to qualify for registration with a provincial association to gain a certificate of practice must meet the requirements specified in the internship program. Internship has been standardized by the Canadian Architectural Certification Board, which oversees education, intern experience and architectural registration exams. Internship involves working for an architect and having a mentor, another architect (possibly retired) who is outside the intern's firm of employment. Registration requires that the work experience cover specified areas of architectural experience. Students can reach this stage by an alternate route, by completing the RAIC Minimum Syllabus Program, which entails qualifying while employed in an architect's office.

Once registered and a member of a provincial association, the young architect becomes one of the approximately eight thousand licenced practitioners in Canada. Registration is not mandatory for certain types of practice. Graduates of architectural programs can work their way into positions of considerable responsibility under registered architects in private practice, or in the public sector's architectural departments, such as municipal, provincial or federal governments. In addition, the unregistered graduate can develop a practice based on small-scale residential and commercial projects under the provincial building code. For example, the

ONTARIO ASSOCIATION OF ARCHITECTS headquarters, Toronto, 1992, Ruth Cawker, Architect.

Ontario Building Code sets certain limits concerning the area (600 square metres), height (three storeys) and occupancy on these projects.

Some graduates may choose further studies, such as urban planning or landscape design. The Royal Architectural Institute of Canada (RAIC) website lists forty-one possible careers. At their meetings, the RAIC has been conducting Consultations and Roundtables on Women in Architecture. Their report from December 2003 states: "Clearly, there is more general awareness that women are a valuable asset to a profession like architecture, and that an organization must be proactive to recruit and maintain women in its folds."

CDP CAPITAL CENTRE, Montreal, 2003, atrium entrance to trading hall, Renée Daoust, Gauthier, Daoust Lestage / Faucher Aubertin Brodeur Gauthier / Lemay et associés.

WOMEN IN ARCHITECTURE TODAY

The six women featured in this chapter received their architecture degrees in the late 1970s to mid-1980s, when women were entering the field in significant numbers. Their experience reflects the range of work open to women architects across Canada: Harriet Burdett-Moulton in Halifax; Renée Daoust in Montreal; Janna Levitt in Toronto; Donna Clare in Edmonton; Jane Pendergast in Calgary; and Joyce Drohan in Vancouver. The text is based on the architects' statements on their own design work and their thoughts on the challenges women face in the field of architecture. Photographs of their work illustrate the chapter.

HARRIET BURDETT-MOULTON finished her B.Arch. degree in 1976 at the Technical University of Nova Scotia in Halifax (now part of Dalhousie University); she also has a degree in Environmental Design from TUNS. Her biggest challenge was finding a job after she graduated, "since not many Halifax firms took a woman seriously." She believes that the profession has become more receptive to women at the entry level in recent years. In large firms, however, only a small number of women hold management positions. As Burdett-Moulton writes: "I think that the current discrimination is more from the architectural firms than from the construction industry or the trades. As in any traditionally male-dominated profession, a female gains credibility in direct proportion to her ability to adopt male mannerisms and to dress the part. A female architect with blond curly hair, blue eyes and dressed in pink but with an IQ of 152 will have a hell of a battle."

Burdett-Moulton considers her most significant project to be the planning of the town of Natuashish, Labrador, for the Innu community that moved from Davis Inlet. As she writes, "It is the only project that I have been involved in where the end users participated in all stages of the planning process. The people tramped the land and showed the consultants where they wanted to locate various aspects of the community and why. They located the school for the views, recognized natural topography suitable for traditional play, and located the sewage lagoon because of its visual screening from the community and directions of the prevailing winds. As project architect, I participated in all of their decisions and directed some of the discussions, but the people made their choices, and they were good choices. At the end of the Community Planning process, the Innu were pleased with their decisions and felt empowered. I felt I was able to give something back in some small way to my roots."

With a practice ranging from the Maritimes to the Arctic, Burdett-Moulton listed some of the specific challenges architects face in the Eastern Arctic that make it more difficult to design and deliver a finished product than working in southern Canada.

Sealift All the building materials that are delivered to rural and remote places with only a sea connection can be delivered only when the water is ice-free. That means that all design and tendering must be completed between February and the end of April or the material cannot be shipped. Paints are classified as dangerous goods, so finish schedules must be completed before the sealift because the paint must be shipped by boat. Some communities have only one sealift per year.

Climate Cold temperatures cause materials to react differently than in southern Canada. Vinyl siding, for example, shatters in low temperatures if there is minimal impact. Severe temperature differentials cause different materials to expand and contract at different rates. Caulking and roofing materials are affected. Low humidity causes glue to dry out and tiles to lift; it also causes warping in kiln-dried wood and glue in furniture to lose its adhesive qualities. Buildings

(LEFT) D.N. SALLUVINIQ GYMNASIUM, Resolute Bay, Northwest Territories, 1990; **(RIGHT) SENIOR CITIZENS' HOUSING**, Iqaluit, Nunavut, 1992, Harriet Burdett-Moulton, Architect.

are elevated to allow snow to pass underneath, preventing drifting around doors. Wind-driven snow is similar to sand in that it is quite corrosive when crystalline. In very cold temperatures, the snow particles are as fine as dust and can be very invasive. Permafrost often restricts the foundation options. Steel pipe piles are the most common foundation system. Concrete is limited to areas where it is economical to install thermosyphons under the concrete to keep the ground permanently frozen.

Sun Angles Buildings should look good and be recognizable in the darkness, which may last a few months in High Arctic communities. Effective lighting has to be designed and located without causing undue light pollution. The sun circles the horizon at a low angle, so the sun can shine horizontally into a room. There is no vertical vegetation for shade or noise screening.

St. Jude's Cathedral in Iqaluit is one of Burdett-Moulton's favourite projects. The original cathedral, designed by Ron Thom, was destroyed by fire in 2005. The new building respects the igloo-inspired design of the original, while enlarging the footprint. It had to address the acoustical problems inherent in a dome structure. The groundbreaking ceremony for the new cathedral was held in June 2007.

JOYCE DROHAN graduated from University of Toronto's School of Architecture in 1978. She believes that many people starting out in architecture have issues with confidence, but it seems to be more prevalent among women. As she says, "There are many larger-than-life personalities in the design professions – not just the stars but those aspiring to be stars. For someone who was relatively shy, it was a constant struggle to make my voice heard." Over the years, Drohan built a solid reputation with a multitude of complex community projects in Vancouver and environs. "Leading multidisciplinary teams, dealing directly with clients, mentoring and teaching in architecture and urban design, chairing the Vancouver and the University of British Columbia design panels, and participating in public forums on architecture have all contributed to my confidence."

Drohan credits her early work in Toronto with giving her both experience and confidence. "My good fortune was to begin my career with James A. Murray, a Toronto pioneer in thoughtful

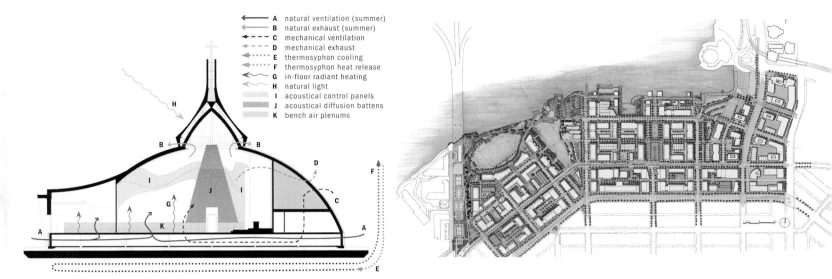

(LEFT) ST. JUDE'S CATHEDRAL, Iqaluit, Nunavut, 2007, section drawing, Harriet Burdett-Moulton, Architect; **(RIGHT) SOUTHEAST FALSE CREEK,** Vancouver, plan for the 2010 Olympic athletes' village, Joyce Drohan with Norm Hotson and Graham McGarva.

A natural ventilation (summer)
B natural exhaust (summer)
C mechanical ventilation
D mechanical exhaust
E thermosyphon cooling
F thermosyphon heat release
G in-floor radiant heating
H natural light
I acoustical control panels
J acoustical diffusion battens
K bench air plenums

mixed-use and community-based projects and the long-time editor of *Canadian Architect* magazine. A talented, warm and often self-effacing man, Jim gave me the opportunity to do my own projects right out of school. As a young graduate, it was invigorating to bring a project to the office and to follow it through from initial design through construction. But perhaps most importantly, I liked the way he thought about projects and their larger urban design implications. This has influenced me to this day."

This foundation served her well in Vancouver, where she has pursued major public buildings and development plans. The key challenge for any architect, she says, is "believing in what you are doing and being patient and persistent enough to see it through the minefields and roller-coaster rides you encounter on any complex architectural project."

As for women in particular, she writes that in recent years women architects are balancing their professional work with personal and family needs, and that the industry has had to adjust to accommodate them. She believes this has offered more flexibility to many men in the profession as well. "In my case, this balance was achieved later than I would have liked. Sometimes I think this has to do with the period in which I joined the profession." Drohan is encouraged by women such as Patricia Patkau: "She demonstrates that an international reputation does not automatically call for a larger-than-life persona. With her quieter, more considered demeanor, she effectively communicates the complexities of design through a style both engaging and rigorous. My hope is for more women in architecture to build a critical public presence, broadening the understanding of architecture and increasing diversity in modes of practice."

Drohan believes that women bring an important perspective to architecture. "Many choose not to be in the spotlight and often miss the opportunity for public acclaim. I believe the smart firms recognize this and encourage and train women to optimize their unique skills in collaboration, client relations and an architecture that is thoughtful and humane. As the profession evolves, my hope is that more women principals might establish in their own firms environments where these unique skills can be channelled to benefit the design and delivery of architecture."

Two projects have been especially significant in her career: Southeast False Creek development plan and Richmond City Hall. They have similarities "as critical steps forward in sustainability,

(LEFT) ROTARY CENTRE FOR THE ARTS, Kelowna, B.C., 2002, Joyce Drohan, Hotson Bakker (HBA); **(RIGHT) RICHMOND CITY HALL,** Richmond, B.C., 2000, Meeting House galleria from north court, Joyce Drohan, HBA/KPMB.

urban design and architecture for two communities responding to unprecedented growth in the Lower Mainland."

The first is Vancouver's official development plan for Southeast False Creek, which the city invited Drohan and two other prominent local architects to design. It will be a community for 14,000 people that will serve as the athletes' village for the 2010 Olympics. "As an architect committed to a more comprehensive approach to sustainable design, I found this was a wonderful opportunity to work from the city scale down to the details of the public realm, ensuring that sustainability figured strongly in every aspect. It reaffirmed my belief that architects are essential to the discussion of city building, bringing skills and vision to craft high-quality public space using built form. Perhaps more importantly, as many cities strive to deliver on sustainability and arrest urban sprawl, Southeast False Creek provides a model demonstrating that increased density can be accommodated without sacrificing liveability."

Richmond is a rapidly urbanizing community just south of the city of Vancouver. Richmond City Hall, which opened in 2000, provides a critical first step in repairing this city's car-based fabric. The project replaces one of many surface parking lots edging the city's main street with an ensemble of buildings, gardens and landscaped courtyards that set a fresh new standard for civic design. As Drohan says, "It demonstrates how a broad mandate for sustainability can be seamlessly woven through a contemporary expression of Northwest design. Before the days of LEED (Leadership in Energy and Environmental Design), Richmond City Hall became the poster child for the federal government's Commercial Buildings Incentive Program (CBIP), an initiative to encourage sustainable design."

As project architect, Drohan worked with two award-winning design firms, Hotson Bakker in Vancouver and Kuwabara Payne McKenna Blumberg (KPMB) in Toronto. "This evolved into a huge benefit for the building, weaving the West Coast sensibilities of one firm (including a solid understanding of sustainable design) with the very fine modernist design skills of the other. Managing a talented team, a building committee comprised of the entire City Council, user groups for every city department from traffic to social services, and a heavy complement of expert consultants to resolve a myriad of technical details for this ambitious design, my human relations skills were forged through this process."

The Rotary Centre for the Arts in Kelowna, B.C., holds a special place in Drohan's portfolio of projects. She enjoyed working

(LEFT) **RICHMOND CITY HALL** is a fine example of sustainable design. (Left) Meeting House and Council Chamber at south terrace water garden; (centre) galleria interior, Joyce Drohan, HBA/KPMB; **(RIGHT) CDP CAPITAL CENTRE,** Montreal, 2003, Renée Daoust, Gauthier, Daoust Lestage/Faucher Aubertin Brodeur Gauthier/Lemay et associés.

with "this small but determined community to create a colourful cultural hub within the city's growing Arts Precinct. As project architect for the facility, I spent many months flying to Kelowna on the rocking-horse flights of Air BC and many weekends in workshops with the building committee."

Budgets were tight for transforming a fruit growers' warehouse into a centre for the visual and performing arts. "Nevertheless, this creative group found ways to support the architectural whimsy and delight that gives this building its distinct personality. Nowhere is this more fully realized than in the double-curved roof and dynamic timber structure of the main public gathering space. This bright, exuberant space is used intensively for a wide assortment of cultural and social events and celebrations. It also acts as a generous anteroom to the centre's 320-seat performance theatre, multiple arts studios and public gallery." This was a period of creative freedom for Drohan. Having just completed the demanding process of delivering Richmond City Hall, she experienced the design of the Centre for the Arts as fluid and relaxing. "It was also a chance to have some fun, which I believe the completed building reflects."

RENÉE DAOUST graduated from University of Montreal's School of Architecture in 1984 and completed a master's degree in Urban Design in 1986. In her experience, the challenges presented to a woman entering the profession are not substantively different from those facing her later in her career. "The primary goal remains the delivery of thorough and rigorous professional services and the development of expertise. In hindsight, a desire to succeed, a passion for the profession and especially a tenacity towards my ideas proved to be essential in the early years of my career, as they still are today."

She believes that the profession has become more receptive to women but their treatment as equals has yet to be achieved. Women in leadership positions have a different management style, "creating some turmoil among fellow architects. A period of adaptation might be required. The end is definitely worth the trouble, the idea being to work towards having a different managerial approach accepted as equally valid."

In terms of recognition, Daoust notes that women do not publicly take credit for their creations as clearly as men do, "leading to a sometimes frustrating distancing phenomenon, where women creators step to the side or are simply pushed aside as projects

(LEFT) CDP CAPITAL CENTRE, Montreal, 2003, the Parquet, a nine-storey atrium; (RIGHT) QUARTIER INTERNATIONAL DE MONTRÉAL, SQUARE VICTORIA, 2004, Renée Daoust, Daoust Lestage / Provencher Roy et Associés / Béïque Thuot Legault.

reach completion. Without resorting to the same male strategies, it is up to women to establish their place in a world still dominated by men by defining for themselves new promotional tools, of which this publication is an example."

Daoust continues: "Unfortunately there remains, although to a lesser extent, a form of latent misogyny where the female approach to creation still disturbs and provokes. In certain particular cases, the acceptance of a woman's ideas by male colleagues may require more effort. A woman's victory in such a situation constitutes one of the most satisfying experiences, given the energy that went into the process. A desire to keep on fighting these battles is essential in order to abolish one by one these preconceived ideas which should not exist today. One is also forced to note the closed culture in some circles of clients towards women architects, contributing to the enduring power of the old boys' club. Some battles are under way that will only be won by the next generation of women."

She believes that women will play an increasingly important role as the profession is globalized. She asks: "What place will women have in this new equation, even in countries where they are not granted the liberties that we have here? Will world-renowned female architects know how to break through the cultural diktats imposed on women in order to create signature projects? Will they open doors for future aspiring women architects? These are all noble challenges facing women architects in the future."

Daoust Lestage, the firm in which Renée Daoust is a founding partner, was established in 1988 with the stated goal of abolishing the walls between the various disciplines related to design, such as urban design, architecture, landscape architecture and interior design. Daoust writes: "The scope of the firm's practice therefore ranges from the scale of the city to the scale of the object. The firm's interventions are deeply anchored in their settings and defined by a timeless simplicity that will allow projects to age better than trendy architectural gestures."

The firm's most significant project is undoubtedly the Quartier international de Montréal and the central building there, the CDP Capital Centre. This impressive urban renewal project embodies Daoust Lestage's approach. The Quartier international de Montréal allows the reconnection of the urban fabric between two of the most significant areas of the city: Old Montreal and the business district.

(LEFT) **LAC-DES-ÉCORCES RÉSIDENCE,** Barkmere, Quebec, 1998, exterior and interior; **(RIGHT) PREMIER-LAC-DU-NORD RÉSIDENCE,** Quebec, 2005, lakeside elevation, Renée Daoust, Daoust Lestage.

Reweaving history into the business city centre proved to be a major challenge. Through the creation of north-south public spaces and the reconnection of underground links, the area now offers "a high-quality living environment that has generated since its creation a real estate return on the investment twenty times greater than the initial costs linked to this urban operation."

Three public spaces were created: the University Street axis, reflecting the colours of the international mosaic; Victoria Square, celebrating its historical roots through the reinstatement of the statue of Queen Victoria and tree-lined avenues; and Place Jean-Paul Riopelle, a public square featuring a sculpture by Quebec artist Jean-Paul Riopelle with water and fire elements.

The CDP Capital Centre was born of the desire to group the institution's 1,500 employees under one roof, "into an intelligent building that would integrate a series of sustainable development strategies and favour synergy between all the employees." This bridge building spans over two city blocks in the heart of the Quartier international. In continuity with the overall conceptual gesture of the Quartier, the building becomes the east-west link between the area's two major public spaces, Victoria Square and Place Jean-Paul Riopelle.

The building's signature space, the Parquet, is a light-filled nine-storey atrium organizing the entire building's horizontal and vertical circulation patterns. Entirely glazed, the building allows an optimal penetration of natural light to lower energy costs. "A neutralizing double-skin and narrow floorplates punctuated by atriums glazed in reflecting surfaces are some of the numerous strategies integrated into the building's design to increase its thermal performance and offer each user a source of natural light."

Daoust's favourite projects are residential. "As an exercise in total design, the creation and construction of a house implies an intrinsic understanding of a client's values, his or her lifestyle, personality and core beliefs. The psychology underlying each space must mirror the client's expectations. Therein lies the challenge for the architect. The opportunity to mould an environment based on a client's prescriptions (prescriptions that evolve as the dialogue between client and architect unfolds) remains one of the most enriching tasks there is." Two of Daoust's private houses are featured on this page: Lac-des-Écorces Résidence and Premier-Lac-du-Nord Résidence.

GALT MUSEUM AND ARCHIVES expansion, Lethbridge, Alberta, 2006, Jane Ferrabee Pendergast, Kasian.

JANE FERRABEE PENDERGAST graduated from University of Toronto's School of Architecture in 1985. She recalls: "In the years I was at school I faced skepticism and was probably subject to more rigour than my male counterparts. I learned to be more forthright and less sensitive – attributes that are necessary in the professional world regardless of who you are. As a woman in architecture you absolutely must keep in touch with who you are, what you want out of your life, and then be prepared to be flexible to get there. It is a profession with many facets so there are many, many choices past a certain point – particularly past the point of registration as an architect. The trick is to make the choices that make the most of your talents and give you pleasure."

Pendergast notes that the construction industry and our society as a whole have become more receptive to women architects. These societal shifts, coupled with a buoyant economy and the development of new technology to support the profession, have brought about the greatest changes. As women attain positions of influence, "our different management and communication style gains currency at the construction trailer table or at the boardroom table. We are more confident as our numbers increase. Thankfully it isn't just the enlightened employers who are now rec-

ognizing the value of offering part-time work, maternity leave and other programs to allow women to blend their professional lives with their larger lives."

She believes that women are especially well suited to architectural practice because of its vastness and its ability to shape our future world. "Women are often well equipped to deal with the broader picture. We are inexplicably sensible and yet tolerant in the decisions we make. We are also collaborative and inclusive in our approach, which suits the complex world of architecture. It's enormously fulfilling to love your work. And I insist that architecture need not rob women of their personal lives."

Pendergast became University Architect at the University of Calgary in the spring of 2006. As University Architect, she acts as the client for a number of projects involving architectural teams while leading the development of a campus community plan for this relatively young university. As she describes it: "This is about boldly leading the collaborative efforts of faculty, students, administration, staff, partners and consulting teams towards the making of a memorable place. It is truly about being an ambassador for excellent design, for sustainable decision-making and for the value of both higher academic and professional education."

STRACHAN HOUSE, Toronto, 1996, Janna Levitt, Levitt Goodman Architects: (left to right) trellised "front porch"; central stair in atrium; view into Town Hall. This redesign of a nineteenth-century factory created a range of housing for men and women who had been living on the streets.

Her favourite design projects in the past have been those that are as much about the experience of working with the clients and the design team as the quality of the final product. "Projects frame experiences during their inception, their development, their documentation, their construction and hopefully well into their lives as they are occupied. I loved working simultaneously on the Galt Museum and Archives Expansion for Lethbridge, Alberta, and the New Calgary Humane Society over the years 2002–2005 at Kasian. Our clients, on both projects, were remarkable people with a vision for their communities. Our architectural and engineering teams were dynamic and talented. We had a great time putting it together with every team member leaving an imprint. I believe both buildings are going on to contribute to a more vibrant community."

JANNA LEVITT graduated from University of Toronto's School of Architecture in 1986. She believes that pervasive sexism is the single biggest challenge for women in architecture. "The practice of architecture is by and large very conservative, and this naturally attracts conservative people. Accordingly the assumptions about women – that they, not men, should be the primary caregivers, for example – are played out in the structure of the practice. Job sharing, flexible hours and part-time employment are not encouraged. If a woman takes time off to have a child, it may be viewed as a lack of commitment to the profession. This translates into the type of work women are given in the larger firms, where the accepted view is that women design interiors while the men design real buildings."

In recent years, the profession is becoming more receptive to women as the number of women entering the field increases. In the smaller firms and partnerships, there is more interest in developing alternative ways to structure an architectural practice. As an adjunct professor at the University of Waterloo School of Architecture, Levitt notes that that there are too few women teaching in the architecture schools; to bring about real change in the profession, women need role models, starting within the academic realm.

Strachan House is one of Levitt's most significant projects. This was a project to design housing for adult men and women who were living on the streets. "We interviewed dozens of people who were homeless – at drop-ins, under bridges – about what a place would have to feel like for them to want to move inside and what they didn't like about the shelters that were currently operating in

EUCLID HOUSE, Toronto, 2005, Janna Levitt, Levitt Goodman Architects: (left to right) front exterior; first floor interior (large skylight above stairwell); living room.

Toronto. There were no precedents for this type of housing, and it required a great deal of inventiveness and an honest recalibration personally and professionally about what constituted 'home.' Acknowledging the transition these residents faced, we developed an analogous architectural operation that we called 'bringing the outside in.' In doing so, we developed a seminal project in a new, contemporary typology known as shelter accommodation."

Strachan House is a radical repurposing of a late-nineteenth-century factory building. Each of the three floors has four "houses" made up of four to seven bedrooms and shared washing, kitchen and dining facilities. These are connected along a corridor, or "main street." The trellised "front porch" marks a clear transition between the public space and the private domain. Weekly meetings are held in the Town Hall on the first floor.

Levitt's current favourite project is the Euclid Avenue house where she and her family live. "This is a house built on a typical Toronto lot: 20 feet wide by 130 feet long, a mid-block lot with all the attending challenges. It is a single-family dwelling that offers an alternative model for residential development in the downtown. It provides all the amenities, spatial complexity, flexibility and warmth of a contemporary home with a modest building size (com-

pared to current standards). This modesty is also reflected in the amount of energy required to both build and operate such a house. Strictly speaking, the Euclid house has a zero footprint since all of the roofs are planted. This shadowless imprint is accomplished by designing the house and site as a coherent, working landscape that together reduce consumption while offering the delight of a roof oasis." In concert with the green roofs are other sustainable infrastructure elements such as: on-demand hot water, radiant floor heating, the strategic employment of natural ventilation, planted roofs and stack effect in lieu of air conditioning, on-site storm water management, and the use of local materials.

The Euclid House is easily converted into a two-family home, promoting a flexible use of space and increasing the population density within the existing footprint. It has stimulated discussion about how to build responsibly in a dense urban context.

DONNA CLARE graduated from University of Toronto's School of Architecture in 1987. She does not recall the challenges she faced on entering the profession to be significantly different than any young, inexperienced person, male or female. "The greater challenges for me came as I gained more experience and began

(LEFT) **ROYAL ALBERTA MUSEUM,** Edmonton, model for the renovation and expansion, Phase 1 to be completed in 2010; **(RIGHT) WINSPEAR CENTRE FOR MUSIC,** Edmonton Symphony Orchestra, 1997, Donna Clare, Cohos Evamy.

to take on a more senior project role. Most of my clients are older and male. Gaining their trust is a challenge."

Another challenge, and perhaps the most significant one, is the attitude women face within architectural firms. "Our firm is one of the few larger practices that has female partners, and even here there are challenges. Over the forty-five years the firm has been in practice, only three women have held partnership positions. Partners relate to each other in both formal and informal ways. The informal interactions, while not intentional, often leave the female partners feeling like outsiders. At a recent partners' retreat, a newly appointed female partner turned to me and said, 'I guess I will need to learn how to smoke cigars, play pool and drink Scotch to fit in.'"

Female architects in Alberta, especially at a partnership level, are still few in number. The profession is gradually becoming more receptive but remains very male-oriented. Clare reports an increase in the number of female interns in recent years. "If they stay in the profession, then I think attitudes will change more rapidly."

One of Clare's current projects is the renewal of the Royal Alberta Museum in Edmonton. The existing building will be expanded and renovated, and the entire site has been re-imagined with innovative landscaping. The museum site links the city to the north with the North Saskatchewan River Valley to the south. Cohos Evamy, where Clare is a partner, is working closely with the landscape architect to blur the lines between inside and outside. A dramatic, articulated roof connects the old and the new, and helps to define visitor circulation. When completed, the museum will double in size.

The Winspear Centre for Music, home of the Edmonton Symphony Orchestra, is another project of particular significance within the city of Edmonton. The 1,900-seat performance chamber is a natural acoustic venue that contributes to the quality of life in the city. At the other end of the spectrum in Clare's design work is a monastery for a cloistered order of nuns in rural Alberta. "For the women who have chosen this calling, this project – the house, the chapel, the grounds – is their world and as a consequence is perhaps the most significant project I will ever undertake."

The Transalta Arts Barn, located in the Old Strathcona neighbourhood of Edmonton, provides versatile indoor and outdoor performance spaces. It has become a beacon in the community,

(LEFT) TRANSALTA ARTS BARN, Old Strathcona, Edmonton, 2003: **(RIGHT) MARKIN/CNRL NATURAL RESOURCES ENGINEERING FACILITY,** University of Alberta, 2004, Donna Clare, Cohos Evamy.

announcing events on the uplit façade of corrugated metal and the original brick. The industrial aesthetic continues on the interior with exposed ductwork and structural elements. A galleria connects the south and north entrances and encourages pedestrian traffic in this lively theatre district.

Reflecting on her recent projects, she says: "Each project has its moments – the chapel in the Carmelite Monastery, the performance chamber of Winspear Centre, the pre-cast concrete panels of the Natural Resources Engineering Facility and the sense of community at Mother Teresa Elementary School in the inner city come to mind. Where I get the most satisfaction, what keeps me going, is providing the client, the users of the facility, with space that supports their goals and their ambition. When I can understand and give form to their vision and take it beyond to create a memorable place that brings delight to the everyday experience, then I have been successful."

As seen in this chapter, women architects in Canada continue to respond with ingenuity to difficulties and have established independent practices or joined firms that are outstanding in both innovation and integration of previously separate fields such as architecture, engineering, urban planning, landscape architecture and interior design. Daoust Lestage, where Renée Daoust is a principal, is especially well known for large-scale urban revitilization projects that show a sensitivity to community within the public space. Cohos Evamy, where Donna Clare is a partner in the Edmonton office, describes itself as being committed to "a fully integrated interdisciplinary practice." Kasian, where Jane Pendergast worked in the Calgary office before becoming the University Architect for University of Calgary, describes itself as an architecture, interior design and planning firm. All of the women profiled in this chapter, but Joyce Drohan, Janna Levitt and Harriet Burdett-Moulton in particular, are leaders in sustainable design.

As more women architects take on larger and more varied design projects, become partners or principals in architectural firms, and teach at schools of architecture across the country, we are sure to see even more impressive developments in the field of architecture in Canada.

ROYAL ALBERTA MUSEUM, Edmonton, renovation and expansion, Phase 1 to be completed in 2010. Donna Clare with Cohos Evamy. The articulated roof opens up the museum and connects the new galleries to the original structure.

APPENDIX A: **THE STORY BEHIND THE EXHIBIT**

Blanche Lemco van Ginkel

With this publication the story of the early women graduates in architecture at University of Toronto becomes more durably "For the Record." The project started in 1983 when I was planning the Faculty of Architecture's contribution to the Centenary of Women celebration at the University of Toronto. It was pretty obvious that we should focus on the first women to study architecture at the University and make an exhibition of their work.

The professional degree program in architecture was instituted at University of Toronto in 1890, with the degree of Bachelor of Applied Science (replaced by the Bachelor of Architecture in 1923). The first woman to be granted the B.A.Sc. in Architecture (and the first woman graduate in architecture in Canada) was Marjorie Hill, in 1920. Anne Rochon Ford made this discovery by chance when she wrote to Ms. Hill to gather information about her mother, who had been one of the early women graduates of the University.

I initially thought that "early" should be prior to 1940, which was when I entered Architecture at McGill. However, a search of the University Archives produced so few names prior to 1940 that I had to extend the period to 1960, rationalizing that this was a generation – a neat twenty-five years – before the Centenary of 1985.

In February 1984 I invited the alumnae who had graduated between 1920 and 1960 to launch the preparation of an exhibition. By November, a small group of alumnae had decided that they wanted to tell their own story, and I cheerfully turned over to them all the research material that I had collected (with the assistance of then students Cathy Dolgy and Pauline Fowler).

Although all of these alumnae had some experience in the practice of architecture, relatively few had a lengthy full-time professional career in the field. But I believe that most of them would agree that their education in architecture stood them in good stead in other pursuits and activities.

An education in architecture involves a wide range of knowledge in both arts and sciences; requires a high degree of integration, analysis and synthesis; and the distillation of knowledge and experience through imagination and visual acuity. I, for example, wrote and produced a film – as have several other architects. Marjorie Hill did practice architecture, but during the lean years of the Depression she applied the same intelligence and skill as a weaver, glovemaker and graphic designer. Among the most rewarding experiences for me in working on this project was an acquaintance with Marjorie Hill, through correspondence and long telephone calls. I had been refused employment early in my career because I was a woman. Consequently, I particularly admired and was humbled by Marjorie Hill who, a generation before me, had pursued her professional life with such fortitude, resourcefulness and good humour.

Women entered the profession of architecture much earlier and in greater numbers in other countries. The knowledge of those pioneers and their achievements sustained many of us in Canada who were not completely accepted in the profession. Although by 1960 there were several women practicing architecture across Canada, the women in the exhibition were representative of the field in those early years and thus *For the Record*, the book, is instructive and may be inspiring to a younger generation. It also should be of enduring value to scholars and to those interested in the history of the Canadian people, dealing as it does with "neglected" leaders.

Blanche Lemco van Ginkel, C.M., FRAIC, RCA, Hon.FAIA, graduated with a Bachelor of Architecture from McGill University in 1945. She received her master's of City Planning at Harvard in 1950. She has been a partner in van Ginkel Associates since 1958 and was Dean of Architecture at the University of Toronto from 1977 to 1982. She is a past president of the Association of Collegiate Schools of Architecture, and a founding officer of the Corporation of the Urbanists of Quebec. In all of these, she was the first woman.

APPENDIX B: THE ORIGINAL EXHIBIT

Mary Clark and Lennox Grafton

"FOR THE RECORD" opened on September 16, 1986, in the School of Architecture Gallery, University of Toronto. **(RIGHT)** Joan Grierson speaking at the opening of the exhibit; Dean Peter Wright and Mary Clark stand to the right.

In the autumn of 1984, the "For the Record" exhibit committee held a meeting of women who had graduated between 1920 and 1960; fourteen of us attended. We decided that the exhibit would focus on the directions in which our professional training had led us. The faculty generously provided space and facilities, and volunteers signed on with expertise in fundraising and public relations, layout and reproduction. With help from university archives and from architectural firms, families and friends, and with the persistence of determined researchers, we unearthed and assembled our exhibit material. This process took two years.

Our research identified four women who deserve special mention, although none of them graduated in architecture in this country. One was Mary Anna Kentner, the first woman to enroll in architecture in Canada in 1916, at the School of Practical Science, University of Toronto. Kentner had originally graduated in Modern Languages, after which she taught in a rural school in Alberta for two years and then travelled abroad. It appears she was accepted into the architecture program as a second-year student before contracting flu in the epidemic of 1918. In any case, she did not return to complete her course.

Another pioneer was Sylvia Grace Holland. Born in England, she arrived in 1926 in Victoria, British Columbia, with her Canadian husband, Frank. Both were qualified architects who had attended the Architectural Association in London. They had returned to Frank's home in Victoria, set up a practice, and were parents of two children when Frank Holland died suddenly. Sylvia Holland continued the practice. Records show that in 1933 she was the first woman to register with the Architectural Institute of British Columbia. However, one of the Holland children was sickly,

(LEFT TO RIGHT) Ruthetta Reiss, Natalie Liacas, Joanna Ozdowski and Isobel Stewart looking at the scrapbooks. **(LEFT TO RIGHT)** Dama Bell, Lennox Grafton, Audrey Christie and Ann Malott at an evening reception hosted by Blanche Lemco van Ginkel.

and in 1936 the family moved to California. State regulations there required Holland to requalify in order to practice architecture; instead, she found work as a commercial artist with Universal Films. In 1938, Sylvia Holland was hired by Walt Disney, for whom she worked on many projects including *Fantasia* and *Bambi.* She later became a freelance artist and continued to live in California until her death in 1957.

In 1914, Alexandra Biriukova was awarded a degree in architecture in Petrograd, Russia, then fled with her family to Rome at the time of the Russian Revolution. There, she studied at the Royal Superior School of Architecture under Arnold Foschini, a noted Italian architect. In 1929, she came to Toronto, where a sister was teaching art at Upper Canada College. Her first commission is thought to have been the interior design of a Russian Orthodox church. Her next commission was the Toronto residence of the Group of Seven painter Lawren Harris. Construction on the Harris residence began in 1931, the year Biriukova registered with the Ontario Association of Architects. When the Depression effectively put an end to her career as an architect, Biriukova (who resigned from the OAA in 1934) trained as a

tuberculosis nurse at the Free Toronto Hospital for the Consumptive Poor. She worked there until her retirement in the 1960s, and died in 1967.

Elma Laird apprenticed in Brantford, Ontario. After a business college education, she worked for two contracting firms in Brantford. Around 1920, Laird went to work in the office of F.C. Bodley, Architect. Her drafting began once her typing was finished. The work was largely residential: her employer would give her a rough idea of requirements and Laird was to take it from there. She did not meet with clients herself, which apparently suited her. To his credit, F.C. Bodley helped Laird to obtain the necessary papers and register with the OAA in 1932. Regrettably, the office closed shortly thereafter, one more casualty of the Depression. Elma Laird continued, for many years, to pay her annual OAA fees "just in case." After 1934, however, and until her retirement, she worked as a secretary at a stationery firm.

At this time, two paths led to OAA registration: one through apprenticeship (as with Elma Laird), and the other through university training. When the first woman graduated from the University of Toronto program in 1920, the architectural course was four

ON THE OPENING DAY OF THE "FOR THE RECORD" EXHIBIT: (left to right) Dama Bell, Joan Grierson, Natalie Liacas, Lennox Grafton, Joanna Ozdowski, (back) Peg Christie, (front) Ruthetta Reiss, Monica Nomberg, Mary Clark (back), Ann Malott, Kay Irvine, Isobel Reeves, Shelagh Rounthwaite, Audrey Christie.

years in length. In 1928, a fifth year was added, and by 1930, there were further registration requirements. For new graduates, this involved two additional years of practical experience. By 1960 (the last year included in the exhibit), there were six architectural schools at Canadian universities, and from these a total of ninety-seven women had graduated.

The 1986 exhibit profiled twenty-eight women, organized by their date of graduation from the School of Architecture. These profiles were in turn grouped into decades to offer some general context, both national and international. All attended the School of Architecture at the University of Toronto between 1918 and 1960, and all were products of the same architectural education system. Admission was based solely on provincial senior matriculation exams, with requirements in specific areas such as mathematics and physics. No consideration was given to artistic ability or to other interests.

It was not until 1957 that new theories regarding the education of architects would begin to alter the direction of the program. The paths of these twenty-eight women present a perspective on many interesting changes in the world and in the application of their architectural training.

The Exhibit Committee: Audrey Christie '54, Mary Clark '58, Lennox Grafton '50 and Joan Grierson '48.

APPENDIX C: SURVEY OF CANADIAN REGISTERED WOMEN ARCHITECTS 1997–1998

In 1997, the For the Record Committee sent questionnaires to 200 women architects, in both large and small practices, who were registered in the provincial associations across the country. The three-question survey asked about the workplace, how they kept current in the field, and their views on the profession.

Eighty responded. Their replies showed that 18 were sole proprietors, 17 worked as partners, 14 within a firm, 5 in the government and 10 in teaching and research. Their specialties involved residential work, health-care facility design, furniture design, innovative housing, energy conservation, lighting research, and theatre and film work. While their perspectives and experiences vary widely, some common themes emerged in their responses.

The opportunity to work creatively was by far the most commonly cited reason these women gave for their satisfaction with the profession. "I get to solve an ever-changing range of problems, put the solutions in practice and move on to something else," said one. Many expressed the excitement of seeing individual projects take shape. They spoke of the pleasure of walking through a building of their own design with a satisfied client. This joy and satisfaction were set against a background of long hours and hard, hard work.

Among the concerns, many women mentioned the danger of getting stuck in a large firm doing "assembly-line architecture." In small firms, some women lamented the amount of the time spent on bookkeeping and invoicing. Another concern was the increasing volume of documentation required to cope with more stringent liability insurance.

The lack of public respect for the profession came up again and again in the responses. One described how depressing it was to find that the public has so little knowledge of the profession. Another found that clients did not respect the time and skill involved in a project; there is more to it than "drafting some plans."

One cited the impact of nonprofessionals, such as builders who work without an architect.

The struggle to generate adequate income received much attention. The profession is extremely sensitive to any downturn in the economy. Few new buildings are commissioned during a recession, and even major renovations are put on hold. One view was that the financial compensation does not reflect the difficulty and complexity of the work. In addition, in many offices the practice seems to regard unpaid overtime as the price one pays to produce good design.

A significant number of respondents had taken on other work, such as teaching architecture on either a full- or part-time basis. Some saw their academic work as a good way to keep up with technical developments in the field. Most relied on the programs held by their provincial associations, conventions, networking and constant reading.

Can a woman combine a successful career in architecture with parenting? The survey found significant divergence of opinion on this issue. Some said they had found it especially difficult to remain active in architecture while their children were young. "The workaholic culture is destructive to family life," said one. Others noted that the birth of children tended to occur just as a woman was being given more responsibility in a firm. Taking maternity leave at this stage, or working part-time, might reduce chances for advancement.

By contrast, several replied that their architectural practice had made it possible for them to maintain their career while raising children. "I have a small practice with a few regular clients," said one woman. "This situation I find absolutely ideal in that it allows me the flexible schedule to balance family needs with professional and career development." Another woman echoed this sentiment, saying, "Women who are able to start their own practice will have the flexibility to enjoy working and a family if they wish." Others mentioned changing attitudes, flexible hours, and the increasing availability of day care as factors in explaining why it is now possible to maintain a full-time career in addition to family responsibilities.

It may be significant that a quarter of the respondents were married to architects. It is plausible that for some women, having a husband in the same line of work might make it easier to share both professional and family responsibilities more fully. On the other hand, when work is scarce, having both partners in the same business makes financial pressures more acute. The survey showed that 13 had been divorced, 52 were married and the number of children totalled 93.

The survey reflected a wide range of opinion on prejudice against women in the profession. "If one likes architecture as a profession," said one woman, "it is as great for women as it is for men, especially now that gender prejudices are substantially reduced from what they were when I studied and started to practice." Another said, "I believe there are the same opportunities for women as for men." Some women stated that they personally had not experienced prejudice, while for others it was a problem that arose on occasion but was ordinarily not a factor. In terms of getting work, one woman observed, "It is possible to succeed. Private development is still a male world, but the situation in institutional settings and private residential work is improving."

Many women reported that although gender bias was not an everyday issue, it did emerge in combination with other problems. For example, during an economic downturn, women might be the first to be laid off. As well, in the early years of their career, a number of women said that they had been slotted into narrow aspects of projects, such as interior design, while male colleagues in the same firm were much more likely to be given scope. As one woman viewed it, "Women will still be regarded as designers, not as builders of buildings."

Keeping up with technical developments, such as CAD, computer-aided design, was difficult for all architects educated before the mid-1980s. Some women reported that male colleagues were more likely to receive ongoing training at company expense. Learning to use the computer and navigate the Internet had to be done on one's own time in many cases. Most offices did not have a budget for training. It is now part of the university curriculum.

Some expressed enthusiasm for the education itself. What is learned lasts a lifetime in terms of perception, interest and awareness. The method of thinking and the steps taken in the design process can be transferred to other disciplines – or to life in general.

All in all, the picture that emerged from the survey was of a profession with an uncertain future. One woman wrote about the dangers of "degenerating into handmaidens of the development industry." Many sought changes in attitudes, such as leadership on environmental and urban issues. "Women will have to reinvent the profession by pushing changes in mentalities," said one respondent. Another wrote, "Women in general are not as easily trapped by the 'genius' complex as are their male colleagues. Thus, they are more open to change and to a smaller practice." In the words of another woman, "Architecture is a profession that has some serious soul-searching and reconfiguring to do in the near future." But she added: "I think women are wonderfully adaptable on the whole and will fare well. I hope we will play an active part in the reshaping of the profession."

Many thanks to all the women who participated in this survey:

Ellen Vera Allen (Toronto, ON)

Laura Helena Arpiainen (Vancouver, BC)

Josée Aubry (Chicoutimi, QC)

Yvette Bernard-Jaffart (Rosemère, QC)

Helen Avini Besharat (Vancouver, BC)

Myriam Blais (Quebec City, QC)

Dianne Bourgeois-VanDommelen
  (Dieppe, NB)

Harriet Burdett-Moulton (Dartmouth, NS)

Elisa Beatrice Brandts (Shelburne, ON)

Linda Brock (Vancouver, BC)

M. Jane Burgess (Toronto, ON)

Rachel Burton (Prince George, BC)

Serena S. Y. Chan (Shatin, Hong Kong)

Linda Chapman (Ottawa, ON)

Pamela Charlesworth (Victoria, BC)

Betty Shuk Kit Chee (Toronto, ON)

Pamela Jean Cluff (Toronto, ON)

Teresa Coady (Vancouver, BC)

Elizabeth Langley Davidson
  (Toronto, ON)

Elizabeth Dechert (Edmonton, AB)

Ludmila Marie Dejmek (Cambridge, ON)

Evelyne Deschamps (Quebec City, QC)

Barbara Anne Dewhirst (Toronto, ON)

Elizabeth Ann Doherty (Ottawa, ON)

Zoya Duba (Montreal, QC)

Claire Dussault (Quebec City, QC)

Mary Jane Finlayson (Toronto, ON)

Eileen Margaret Fletcher (Revelstoke, BC)

Lucie Fontein (Ottawa, ON)

Andrea Hajdo Forbes (Richmond, BC)

Julia Gersovitz (Montreal, QC)

Cindy Gibson (Winnipeg, MB)

Kelly Lee Gilbride (Deep River, ON)

Catherine Green (Winnipeg, MB)

Lynda Jane Hansen (Ottawa, ON)

Karen Hillel (Victoria, BC)

Mary Jo Hind (Dundas, ON)

Barbara Humphreys (Manotick, ON)

Patricia L. Hurley (Longueuil, QC)

Mary Louise Jaansalu (Orleans, ON)

Carol-Jean Kleinfeldt (Toronto, ON)

Kathleen Laliberté (Charlesbourg, QC)

Gail E. Lamb (Lucan, ON)

Phyllis Lambert (Montreal, QC)

Anne Larose (Noranda, QC)

Florence Levine (Vancouver, BC)

Natalka Lubiw (Vancouver, BC)

Marie-Paule MacDonald (Waterloo, ON)

Brenda L. MacKneson (Toronto, ON)

Vivian Manasc (Edmonton, AB)

Ann Emily March (Saskatoon, SK)

Elizabeth Marcovici (Montreal, QC)

Cristina Marghetti (Vancouver, BC)

Derby Lynn Martin (Winnipeg, MB)

Eva Matsuzaki (Vancouver, BC)

Karen McAuley (Montreal, QC)

Nicole Milette (Montreal, QC)

Erica Moghal (Mississauga, ON)

Catherine Nasmith (Toronto, ON)

Margaret Elizabeth Beaton Newell
  (Victoria, BC)

Ana Nunes (Sainte-Foy, QC)

Tina Marie Nuspl (Montreal, QC)

Laura O'Neill (Edmonton, AB)

Marie-Claude Parent (Granby, QC)

Jane Pendergast (Calgary, AB)

Helga Woitech Plumb (Toronto, ON)

Nathalie Rhéaume (Quebec City, QC)

Marie-Louise Roy (Boisbriand, QC)

Ingrid Carla Ruthig (Ajax, ON)

Barbara Sankey (Victoria, BC)

Maria Silvia Scandella (Calgary, AB)

Mireille Shebib-Aubé
  (Ville Saint-Laurent, QC)

Teresa Shimbashi (Burnaby, BC)

Natalie C. Smith (Victoria, BC)

Maria Somjen (Halifax, NS)

Nancy Stern (Vancouver, BC)

Natalija Subotincic (St. Pascal, ON)

Susan Turner (Winnipeg, MB)

Cynthia Wahl (Dorval, QC)

Valerie Anne Wilson (Edmonton, AB)

Joanne Wright (Calgary, AB)

Viviana Zothner-Cotic (Toronto, ON)

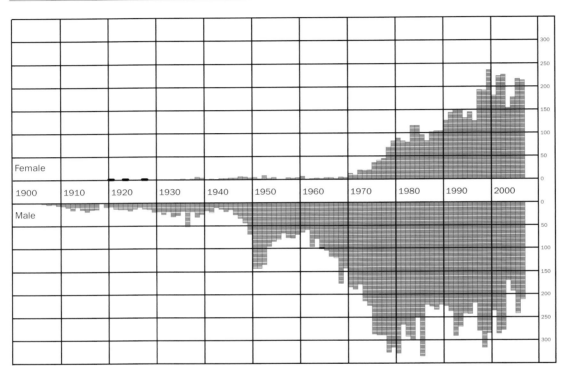

Female

| 1900 | 1910 | 1920 | 1930 | 1940 | 1950 | 1960 | 1970 | 1980 | 1990 | 2000 |

Male

Comparison of Male and Female Graduates

This graph shows the number of graduates from Canadian schools of architecture from 1900 to 2006. The upper bars indicate the number of women to graduate each year; the lower bars show the number of men. It is apparent that the number of women graduates is fast approaching that of men.

The eleven Canadian universities that currently offer a professional degree program in architecture appear in **bold**. Schools of Architecture were established at Canadian universities as follows:

1890 **University of Toronto,** Toronto
1896 **McGill University,** Montreal
1907 École Polytechnique, Montreal
(later part of Université de Montréal)
1913 University of Alberta, Edmonton (closed for two years during the First World War and permanently in 1939)
1918 **University of Manitoba,** Winnipeg
1922 École des Beaux Arts, Quebec City (closed 1936)
1939 **University of British Columbia,** Vancouver

1961 **Université Laval,** Quebec City
1961 Technical University of Nova Scotia, Halifax
(later part of Dalhousie University)
1964 **Université de Montréal,** Montreal
1966 **University of Waterloo,** Waterloo
1968 **Carleton University,** Ottawa
1972 **University of Calgary,** Calgary
2000 **Dalhousie University,** Halifax
2007 **Ryerson University,** Toronto

Canadian universities with professional degrees in Architecture approved by the Canadian Architectural Certification Board (CACB)

University	Undergraduate requirements	Length of Master's/ professional degree	Enrolment in final professional degree	Number accepted into first year	Percentage of women students
University of British Columbia Vancouver, BC	3-year Bachelor of Environmental Science	3 years	136	45	36%
University of Calgary Calgary, AB	3-year Bachelor of Environmental Studies	4 years	74	22	35%
Carleton University Ottawa, ON	4-year Bachelor of Architectural Studies	2 years	59	28	33%
Dalhousie University Halifax, NS	4-year Bachelor of Environmental Design Studies	2 years	93	50–55	42%
Université Laval Quebec City, QC (French language instruction)	3-year Bachelor of Architecture	1.5 years	93	50–60	46%
University of Manitoba Winnipeg, MB	4-year Bachelor of Environmental Science	2 years	121	25	41%
McGill University Montreal, QC	3-year Bachelor of Science in Architecture	1.5 years	88	45	68%
Université de Montréal Montreal, QC (French language instruction)	3-year Bachelor of Science in Architectural Design	1.5 years	126	75	59%
University of Toronto Toronto, ON	Bachelor of Arts (in any discipline)	3.5 years	216	77	46%
University of Waterloo Waterloo, ON	3-year Bachelor of Environmental Science (Coop: alternating study and work terms)	2 years (Coop)	85	55	48%

Data taken from *Architecture Schools*, 7th Edition, published by the Association of Collegiate Schools of Architecture, Washington, D.C., 2003 and the *Guide to Canadian Graduate Schools of Architecture*, published by the Canadian Students Association, 2006. As of September 2007, Ryerson University offers a four-year Bachelor of Architectural Science and a two-year master's degree.

SELECTED RESOURCES

Adam, Peter. *Eileen Gray, Architect/Designer.* New York: Abrams, 1987.

Adams, Annmarie, and Peta Tancred. *Designing Women: Gender and the Architectural Profession.* Toronto: University of Toronto Press, 2000.

Berkeley, Ellen Perry, ed. *Architecture: A Place for Women.* Washington, DC: Smithsonian Institution, 1989.

Bleznakov, Milka. *Soviet Women Architects, 1937: A Bibliographical Guide to Their Work.*

Boutelle, Sara Holmes. *Julia Morgan Architect.* Rev. ed. New York: Abbeville Press, 1995.

Cole, Doris. *Eleanor Raymond, Architect.* Cranberry, NJ: The Art of Alliance Press, Associated University Presses, 1981.

———. *From Tipi to Skyscraper: A History of Women in Architecture.* Cambridge, MA: MIT Press, 1973.

———, and Karen Cord Taylor. *The Lady Architects: Lois Lilley Howe, Eleanor Manning and Mary Almy, 1893–1937.* New York: Midmarch Arts Press, 1990.

Dietsch, Deborah. "Lily Reich." *Heresies 3* (1981): 73-76.

Finnish Association of Women Architects. *Profiles: Pioneering Women Architects from Finland.* Helsinki: Museum of Finnish Architecture, 1983.

Ford, Anne Rochon. *A Path Not Strewn with Roses: 100 Years of Women at the University of Toronto 1884–1984.* Toronto: Women's Centenary Committee, University of Toronto, 1985.

Freedman, Adele. "An Intimate Portrait of the First 'Girl' Architects." *Globe and Mail,* September 20, 1986.

Gillet, Margaret. *We Walked Very Warily: A History of Women at McGill.* Montreal: Eden Press Women's Publications, 1981.

Glaster, Gertrude. "Women Architects in Denmark." *Architekten* 85 (16): 1983.

Hayden, Dolores. *Redesigning the American Dream: Gender, Housing, and Family Life.* New York: Norton, 2002.

———. *The Grand Domestic Revolution: A History of Feminist Designs for American Houses, Neighborhoods and Cities.* Cambridge, MA: MIT Press, 1981.

Kalman, Harold. *A History of Canadian Architecture.* Vols. 1–2. Toronto: Oxford University Press, 1994.

Klodawsky, Fran. "Employment Opportunities for Women in Architecture and Planning: Problems and Prospects." *Womens Bureau: Labour Canada* (1981).

Lorenz, Clare. *Women in Architecture: A Contemporary Perspective.* New York: Rizzoli, 1990.

Patterson, Nancy. "Architecture — Work by Women." *Fifth Column* (Summer 1983).

Rochon, Lisa. *Up North: Where Canada's Architecture Meets the Land.* Toronto: Key Porter, 2005.

Rudberg, Eva. "Women in Architecture." *Arkitektur* (March 1983).

Rybczynski, Witold. *Looking Around: A Journey Through Architecture.* Toronto: Penguin Canada, 1992.

Torre, Susana, ed. *Women in American Architecture: A Historic and Contemporary Perspective.* New York: Whitney Library of Design, 1977.

Walker, Lynne, Gillian Darley, Bebbe Klatt, Beeban Morris, and Stephanie Williams. *Women Architects: Their Work.* London,UK: Sorella Press, 1984.

Weimann, Jeanne Madeline. *The Fair Women: The Story of the Women's Building at the World's Columbian Exposition of 1893.* Chicago: Academy Chicago, 1981.

Women in Architecture Exhibits Committee. *Constructing Careers: Profiles of Five Early Women Architects in British Columbia.* Vancouver, BC: Architectural Institute of British Columbia, 1996.

EDUCATIONAL GUIDES

Association of Collegiate Schools of Architecture. Guide to *Architecture Schools: Comprehensive Guide to Accredited Schools of Architecture in the U.S. and Canada. 7th ed.* Washington, DC: Association of Collegiate Schools of Architecture, 2003.

Camenson, Blythe. *Careers in Architecture.* New York: McGraw-Hill, 2001.

Canadian Architecture Students Association. *Guide to Canadian Graduate Schools of Architecture.* Canadian Architecture Students Association, 2006.

Lewis, Roger K. *Architect? A Candid Guide to the Profession.* 2nd ed. Cambridge, MA: MIT Press, 1998.

Piper, Robert J. *Opportunities in Architecture Careers.* New York: McGraw-Hill, 2006.

WEBSITES

Canadian Architectural Archives
Based at the University of Calgary, this archive's mandate is to collect the work of twentieth-century Canadian architects.
www.caa.ucalgary.ca

Canadian Architectural Certification Board
The first point of contact for graduates from professional programs in architecture in Canada and abroad who plan to become licenced architects in Canada.
cacb.ca

Canadian Centre for Architecture
An international research centre and museum devoted to architecture. Located in Montreal.
www.cca.qc.ca

International Archive of Women in Architecture
Located at the Virginia Polytechnic Institute and State University.
spec.lib.vt.edu/iawa

Royal Institute of British Architects
RIBA produced a report on a fascinating survey on why women leave the field of architecture. The full report is available from this link:
www.riba.org/go/RIBA/Also/Education_2691.html

NATIONAL AND PROVINCIAL ORGANIZATIONS

The Royal Architectural Institute of Canada (RAIC): www.raic.org
Look for the survey on women in the profession:
raic.org/resources_archives/research/womeninarch_e.pdf

Alberta Association of Architects
www.aaa.ab.ca

Architectural Institute of British Columbia
www.aibc.ca

Manitoba Association of Architects
www.mbarchitects.org

Architects Association of New Brunswick
www.aanb.org

Newfoundland Association of Architects
www.newfoundlandarchitects.com

Northwest Territories Association of Architects
www.nwtaa.ca

Nova Scotia Association of Architects
www.nsaa.ns.ca

Ontario Association of Architects
www.oaa.on.ca

Architects Association of Prince Edward Island
www.aapei.com

Ordre des architectes du Quebec
www.oaq.com

Saskatchewan Association of Architects
www.saskarchitects.com

SCHOOLS OF ARCHITECTURE

Canadian Architecture Students Association
www.casa-acea.org
In 2006, CASA published a guide to Canadian schools of architecture.
Available for purchase online.

University of British Columbia
www.arch.ubc.ca
soaadmit@interchange.ubc.ca

University of Calgary
www.evds.ucalgary.ca/programs/arch
info@evds.ucalgary.ca

Carleton University
www.arch.carleton.ca
architecture@carleton.ca

Dalhousie University
www.archplan.dal.ca
arch.office@dal.ca

Laval University
www.arc.ulaval.ca
arc@arc.ulaval.ca

University of Manitoba
www.umanitoba.ca/architecture
architecture@cc.umanitoba.ca

McGill University
www.mcgill.ca/architecture
profdegree.architecture@mcgill.ca

University of Montreal
www.arc.umontreal.ca
dirame@ame.umontreal.ca

Ryerson University
www.ryerson.ca/arch

University of Toronto
www.ald.utoronto.ca
enquiry.ald@utoronto.ca

University of Waterloo
www.architecture.uwaterloo.ca
info@architecture.uwaterloo.ca

ACKNOWLEDGEMENTS

Work on this book has evolved in the years following the initial exhibit. There are many to whom we are very grateful. Two architectural historians helped in the initial stages: Geoffrey Simmons provided wise counsel on organization and Shirley Morriss contributed research material. Laura Stone dealt with photography and Natalka Lubiw assembled the first layouts.

Then there are those without whom this book might not exist. At the University of Toronto Press, the following worked with us over the years: Lawrie Lewis, Beth Earl Rose, Molly Schlosser, Will Reuter and Janet Slaven. Preliminary texts were compiled by Maureen Spratley. Data and translations for the survey were handled by Natalie Liacas and Andrea Kristof. Ruth MacKneson made available her research on women in engineering. Olive Koyama, Sasha Chapman, Sophie Peacock, Bart Hawkins-Kreps, Patricia Post and Pat Holts contributed to early editorial work on the book. We very much appreciated the excellent design work by Janice van Eck, which was adapted to the later format. Mary Clark and Lynne Fox dealt efficiently and patiently with the quagmire of photo permissions. Ruth Gaskill compiled the permissions to create the Photo Credits page for the book. Text revisions were handled by computer wizards Bernice Lester, our "White Knight" Harry Jahn, and last but certainly without equal, Christie Morrison of In Good Order, our administrative assistant.

The profile of Mary Imrie was immeasurably improved by Mary Bramley's photographs. In particular, her documentation of the Harvie House in Calgary led us to feature it both in the opening pages and on the jacket. We'd also like to thank Steven Evans, who generously donated an excellent photograph of the OAA building.

Mary Clark and her daughter, Panya, assembled biographical data in scrapbooks for the exhibit, which were then donated to the University of Toronto Archives. We consulted these scrapbooks closely for the Epilogue. The research for Appendix D was also done by Mary.

We are grateful for the assistance of Dean George Baird at the School of Architecture and Landscape Architecture at the University of Toronto for crucial suggestions on the final chapter. George Baird introduced us to five of the six architects featured in the final chapter.

Harriet Burdett-Moulton (Halifax & Nunavut), Donna Clare (Edmonton), Renée Daoust (Montreal), Joyce Drohan (Vancouver), Janna Levitt (Toronto) and Jane Pendergast (Calgary): these six women were extremely generous with their time, contributing both invaluable information about their own experiences working in architecture and photographic images of some of their recent work for the book.

We salute Blanche Lemco van Ginkel, who was the prime mover behind the exhibition. Blanche continued to encourage us, even after we took the reins, and later, when we decided to build on the exhibit to create this book.

In addition to support from the Canada Council, the Jackman Foundation and the Ontario Association of Architects, the following architectural firms and individuals contributed financially during the research and writing of this book: Adamson Associates, Ferguson Simek Clark, Mathers & Haldenby, Moffat Kinoshita Architects, C.A. Ventin Architect and Zeidler Roberts. Many thanks to one and all.

We would like to extend special thanks to our editor, Meg Taylor, for creative input and unflagging enthusiasm for this project. These attributes were shared by the creative design team at Counterpunch, Linda Gustafson and Peter Ross. Peter's inventive design solutions and attention to detail were deeply appreciated over the course of many page proofs. To the pivotal figure of

Rick Archbold, our heartfelt thanks for his excellent assessment of the project, and for introducing us to Meg.

Thanks to Kirk Howard, Publisher at Dundurn Press, who has championed our book in the publishing world, and to Michael Carroll, Barry Jowett, Jennifer Scott, Marja Appleford, Erin Winzer and the rest of the team at Dundurn. Lloyd Davis created an excellent index.

And finally, thanks to Eva Matsuzaki, who supported the book with comments and a generous Foreword.

For the Record Committee: Joan Burt, Lennox Grafton, Joan Grierson and Natalie Liacas

ACKNOWLEDGEMENTS FOR THE EXHIBIT

"For the Record," an exhibit in recognition of early women graduates in the field of architecture at the University of Toronto, opened on September 16, 1986, at the School of Architecture Gallery. The exhibit was made possible by the expertise and generosity of the following individuals, firms and organizations.

DONORS
Alice Ayer Alison; Beatrice Centner Davidson; Ferguson Simek Clark Inc., Architects and Engineers; Fiberglass Canada; Lennox Grafton; Katharine Jefferys Helm; Ontario Ministry of Citizenship and Culture; Ontario Ministry of Government Services; Ontario Women's Directorate; Isobel Stewart Reeve; Shelagh Macdonnell Rounthwaite; Joan M. Tyrell; Dean Peter Wright, Faculty of Architecture and Landscape Architecture, University of Toronto

SPONSOR
The Architectural Conservancy of Ontario

RESEARCH
Harold Averill, University of Toronto Archives; The Carlisle Family; Douglas Dryer; George Kentner Gooderham; Catherine Green; Robert Hill; Vicky Jakoljevic; Elizabeth Kenny; The Lalor Family; Pamela Manson-Smith, Faculty of Architecture and Landscape Architecture, University of Toronto; Shirley Morriss; Anne Rochon Ford; Audrey Shannon; Doris Newland Tanner; Joan Wagner

PUBLICITY
Audrey Ellard; Colleen Morris, University of Toronto

TIME AND EXPERTISE
Karen Alison; Joan Burt; Audrey Christie; Margaret Christie; Clive Clark; Panya Clark; Jackie Fine; Karen Fleischmann; Blanche Lemco van Ginkel; David Hambleton, Wagg and Hambleton, Architects; Kathleen Irvine; Monique Koningstein; Laurie Lewis, University of Toronto Press; Natalka Lubiw; Ann McIlroy; Martine Mowatt; Joanna Ozdowski; Komola Prabhakar and the office staff, Faculty of Architecture and Landscape Architecture, University of Toronto; Isobel Stewart Reeves; Barbara Sankey; Sandy Smith; Christine Urszenyi; Dean Peter Wright

PHOTOGRAPHY
Lennox Grafton; Lindsay Jackson, The Jackson Klomstad Partnership, Toronto; Gilbert Prioste, Faculty of Architecture and Landscape Architecture, University of Toronto; Tony Sayle

EXHIBIT COMMITTEE
Audrey Christie; Mary Clark; Lennox Grafton; Joan Grierson

PHOTO CREDITS

Every attempt has been made to trace ownership of copyright material in this book and to secure permissions. The publisher would appreciate receiving information on any inaccuracies in the credits for correction in subsequent editions.

FRONT MATTER
Page 1, left, Lennox Grafton; right, executor, Mary Louise Imrie Estate, Provincial Archives of Alberta PR1988.290/180; p. 2, left, Mary Bramley; right, Natalie Liacas; p. 3, left, Lennox Grafton; right, Richard Zaplitney.

PREFACE
Page 10, the British Library.

A SHORT HISTORY OF EARLY WOMEN IN ARCHITECTURE
Page 12, St. Lawrence Parks Commission, Fort Henry; p. 14, left, *Builder* magazine, January 4, 1851; right, National Archives of Canada PA-028772; p. 15, left, Fairmont Le Château Frontenac; right, Public Works Canada; p. 16, left, Hudson River Museum, Yonkers, N.Y.; right, Buffalo and Erie County Historical Society; p. 17, left, James H. Edelen, Sara Holmes Boutelle Papers 141-3-B-38-6, Julia Morgan Collection, Special Collections, California Polytechnic State University; right, Mati Maldre.

THE 1920S
Page 20, chair, courtesy of Knoll, Inc.; car, *Art as Design: Design as Art* by Sterling McIlhany (New York: Van Nostrand Reinhold, 1970); bottom left, © Parks Canada/A. Guindon; bottom centre, City of Edmonton Archives EA-10-740; bottom right, Greta Grey, *House and Home*, 1923; p. 21, left, Bauhaus-Archiv Berlin; right, RIBA Library Photographs Collection; p. 22, top and bottom, University of Toronto Archives; p. 23, top, Tony Sayle, PhotoFor Photography, Victoria, B.C.; bottom left and right, University of Toronto Archives; p. 24, top, courtesy of the Hall Family; bottom, Torontonensis; p. 25, top left, For the Record: Exhibit Committee; top right, Lennox Grafton; bottom left, courtesy of the Hall Family; bottom right, *Toronto Star*; p. 26, top, *Toronto Star*; bottom, and p. 27, all images, *Canadian Homes and Gardens*.

THE 1930S
Page 28, chair, courtesy of Knoll, Inc; car, Volkswagen of America Inc.; bottom left and centre, Royal Architectural Institute of Canada; bottom right, Lennox Grafton; p. 29, left, Royal Architectural Institute of Canada; centre, Archives of Ontario RG 9-7-5-0-5; right, Public Works

Canada; p. 30, top left, courtesy of the B.C. Davidson Family; top right, University of Toronto Engineering Society; bottom, Joan Grierson; p. 31, left top and bottom, courtesy of the B.C. Davidson Family; top right, Lennox Grafton; bottom right, Joan Grierson; p. 32, top, Kevin and Kerry Bell; bottom, University of Toronto Engineering Society; p. 33, top, Kevin and Kerry Bell; bottom, Dama Bell; p. 34, top left, courtesy of the Carlisle Family; top right, Kevin and Kerry Bell; bottom, Jackson Klomstadt Partnership; p. 35, left top and bottom, For the Record: Exhibit Committee; right top and bottom, Jackson Klomstadt Partnership; p. 36, top left, courtesy of the Malott Family; top right, University of Toronto Archives; bottom, GE Canada; p. 37, top, Rockefeller Center Archives; bottom left and right, Royal Architectural Institute of Canada.

THE 1940S
Page 38, chair, courtesy of Herman Miller Inc.; car, Applegate and Applegate; bottom left, Eleanor Raymond Collection, Frances Loeb Library, Harvard Design School; bottom centre, photograph by Otto T. Mallery and Timothy A. Gregg, © 2007 The Frank Lloyd Wright Foundation/Artists Rights Society (ARS), New York/SODRAC, Montreal; bottom right, Royal Architectural Institute of Canada; p. 39, left, Royal Architectural Institute of Canada; right, Tony Archer; p. 40, top, Martha Crase; bottom, University of Toronto Engineering Society; p. 41, top left, Joan Grierson; top right, University of Toronto Engineering Society; bottom, Margaret Dryer; p. 42, top, University of Toronto Engineering Society; bottom, executor, Mary Louise Imrie Estate, Provincial Archives of Alberta PR1988.290/768; p. 43, top and bottom left, executor, Mary Louise Imrie Estate, Provincial Archives of Alberta PR1988.290/180; bottom right, *Saturday Night*; p. 44, top, Mary Bramley; centre and bottom right, executor, Mary Louise Imrie Estate, Provincial Archives of Alberta PR1988.290/28; bottom left, executor, Mary Louise Imrie Estate, Provincial Archives of Alberta PR1988.290/27; p. 45, all images, Mary Bramley; p. 46, top and bottom right, executor, Mary Louise Imrie Estate, Provincial Archives of Alberta PR1988.290/582; bottom left, executor, Mary Louise Imrie Estate, Provincial Archives of Alberta PR1988.290/583; p. 47, top, executor, Mary Louise Imrie Estate, Provincial Archives of Alberta PR1988.290/620; bottom, Mary Bramley; p. 48, top, Gordon, Adrienne & Karen Alison; bottom, University of Toronto Engineering Society; p. 49, top, Lennox Grafton; bottom, Gordon, Adrienne & Karen Alison; p. 50, top, Gordon, Adrienne & Karen Alison; bottom left, *Toronto Star*; bottom right, City of Toronto Archives, Fonds 1231, Item 311; p. 51, top and bottom, Shelagh Rounthwaite; pp. 52–53, Isobel Stewart; p. 54, top, Jean Strange; bottom, Central Mortgage and Housing Corporation (CMHC). Housing Design Part I,

1952. All rights reserved; p. 55, top, Marshall Studios Limited, St. John's, Nfld.; centre and bottom right, Central Mortgage and Housing Corporation (CMHC). Small House Designs–2-Storey, 1952. All rights reserved; bottom left, Central Mortgage and Housing Corporation (CMHC). After Hours, 1954. All rights reserved.; p. 56, top, Clive Clark; bottom, Joan Grierson; p. 57, all images, Joan Grierson; p. 58, top, Joan Grierson; bottom, and p. 59, top and bottom, Ruthetta Kaplan Reiss.

THE 1950S
Page 60, chair, courtesy of Knoll, Inc.; car, Applegate and Applegate; bottom left, photograph by David Heald, © Solomon R. Guggenheim Foundation, New York, © 2007 The Frank Lloyd Wright Foundation/Artists Rights Society (ARS), New York/SODRAC, Montreal; bottom centre, City of Toronto Archives; bottom right, RIBA Library Photographs Collection; p. 61, left, Jeffrey Lindsay, Royal Architectural Institute of Canada; centre, Hellmut W. Schade; right, Royal Architectural Institute of Canada; p. 62, top, Mary Clark; bottom, Lennox Grafton; p. 63, top and bottom, Lennox Grafton; p. 64, left, For the Record: Exhibit Committee; right top, centre, and bottom, Lennox Grafton; p. 65, top and bottom, Lennox Grafton; p. 66, left and top right, Lennox Grafton; bottom right, Natural Resources Canada; p. 67, top, Ventin Group Ltd., Architects; bottom, Lennox Grafton; p. 68, top left and right, courtesy of the Smale Family; bottom left and right, Ventin Group Ltd., Architects; pp. 69–70, Margaret Gisborne Christie; p. 71, top and bottom, Marjorie Shepland; pp. 72–75, Audrey Christie; p. 76, Joan Burt; p. 77, all images, Joan Burt, Architect; p. 78, all images, Richard Zaplitney; p. 79, top left and right, Richard Zaplitney; bottom left and right, Joan Burt, Architect; p. 80, Mary Clark; p. 81, all images, Panda Associates; p. 82, top left and right, and bottom left, Panda Associates; bottom right, Joanna Ozdowski; p. 83, top left, Joanna Ozdowski; right top and centre, Panda Associates; bottom, Lennox Grafton; p. 84, Kathleen Irvine; p. 85, top, Kathleen Irvine; centre left and right, and bottom, J.A. Griffiths of Murray and Murray, Griffiths and Rankin, elevations drawn by Mary Eng; p. 86, top, Clive Clark; bottom, City of Toronto, Urban Development Services; p. 87, top, Mary Clark; bottom left and right, Clive Clark; p. 88, Monica Nomberg; pp. 89–91, Edward Durrell Stone Associates P.C.; p. 92, top, Walter V. Liacas; bottom, Ministry of Government Services; p. 93, all images, Natalie Liacas; p. 94, top and bottom, Ontario Ministry of Tourism; p. 95, drawings by Natalie Liacas; p. 96, top left and bottom, Natalie Liacas; top right, Wallace R. Berry; p. 97, top left and right, Natalie Liacas; bottom, Gordon Grice OAA, FRAIC.

EPILOGUE
Page 101, Steven Evans.

WOMEN IN ARCHITECTURE TODAY
Page 102, Alain Laforest; p. 104, left and right, Harriet Burdett-Moulton; p. 105, left, graphics by FSC Architects & Engineers; right, VIA Architecture/Hotson Bakker Boniface Haden/Stantec Architecture/ PWL Partnership; p. 106, left, Wayne Duchart; right, Martin Tessler; p. 107, left and centre, Martin Tessler; right, Stéphan Poulin; p. 108, left, Stéphan Poulin; right, Daoust Lestage; p. 109, left, Alain Laforest; centre, Mario Dubreuil; right, Vittorio Vieira; p. 110, Kasian Architecture Interior Design and Planning Ltd.; pp. 111–112, Ben Rahn/A-Frame, courtesy of Levitt Goodman Architects; p. 113, left, Ellis Associates (model), Lotus Studio Photography Ltd.; right, Ellis Brothers Photography Ltd.; p. 114, left, Statler Studios; right, Lotus Studio Photography Ltd.; p. 115, Cicada Design, Toronto.

APPENDIX B
Pages 118–120, Lennox Grafton.

INDEX